Fuck

This

Class!

An "appalling" tale of a
District75 New York City Teacher

Sir Cedric QH

Printed in the United States of America

First Printing, 2014

For my mom, Linda

Who not only lifted my chin to the sky, but also my sense of individualism.

TABLE OF CONTENTS

She even thinks that up in heaven
Her class lies late and snores

While poor black cherubs rise at seven
To do celestial chores.

-Countee Cullen

Fuck

This

Class!

An "appalling" tale of a
District75 New York City Teacher

This is a true story and the names have not been changed-- mostly in order to expose the guilty. And you amoebas, you can do what you do best!

Department of Education
Gary Hecht Superintendent

February 12, 2014
Mr. Cedric Hines
Division of Students with Disabilities & English Language
Learners
Probationary Teacher, P226M

Dear Mr. Hines,

On February 12, 2014, my representative, Susan Holtzman, met with you at the District Office. Also present at the meeting was your UFT representative, Jeff Huart, and P226M Principal, Rachelle Klainberg. The purpose of this meeting was to discuss your professional misconduct on February 11, 2014. Specifically, you taught a lesson to your severely cognitively delayed, Autistic, 6:1:1 students on "Jack the Ripper" (attached). The unit of study you were supposed to be teaching your students was on Industrialization; inventions and inventors. You created a teacher made book for your students on "Jack the Ripper" with graphic depictions of violence.

You had the opportunity both prior to responding to this issue and at several points during the meeting to step outside and consult with Mr. Huart.

At the meeting, Ms. Holtzman asked you to explain why you felt Jack the Ripper was an appropriate informational text for 6:1:1 special needs severely cognitively delayed middle school students. In response, you presented numerous documents from what you stated was your "Teaching Fellows Program". The documents did not have any relevance to Ms. Holtzman's question. You also discussed common core and what it expected of the students. You stated that you had taught a previous class on "Forensics" and you then presented a book (attached) that you had used for that lesson. As per Ms. Holtzman and Principal Klainberg, you never explained why you felt that "Jack the Ripper" was a proper topic for your students or the subject area you were trying to teach.

After reviewing your lesson, and your responses at the meeting, I conclude that the topic of your lesson was completely inappropriate and, quite frankly, appalling. Your actions were egregious, and had no appropriate educational value for your students and their cognitive level. You have been provided with instructional supports during the 2013-2014 school year, including an instructional map for teaching your students, mentor training, and additional assistance from both the Assistant Principals and your Principal.

You have refused to or failed to understand the directives you were given.

Based on your extraordinary misconduct, you are hereby discontinued from your probationary service with the DOE, effective March 14,2014. Additionally, I am noting your poor pedagogic performance.Your observations are attached. You have the right to provide me with a written document outlining why I should not discontinue your probationary service. I must receive this information 7 days prior to March 14,2014. Starting immediately, you are to report to 400 1st Avenue, NYC, NY 10010, where you will be assigned a work location until March 14, 2014. Your work hours are 8:00am to 2:50pm, with a 50 minute duty free lunch, which will be assigned when you report. Please report to the School Safety Agent in the Main Lobby upon arrival in the building and she will inform Ms. Holtzman of your arrival.

Sincerely,

Gary Hecht,
Superintendent District 75

Chapter 1:"I gotta get out of here"

As a youth, I never fully learned how to obey—or, to subdue my opinions to the paradigms of society. I just could not act accordingly. My kindergarten teachers rated my "ability to get along with others," as unsatisfactory. That flippant tongue of mine was always a little too slick and I was constantly shown the door. And I demanded too much: I'd curse out a teacher or two in high school for assuming I should accept B's and C's when they knew damn well my work demanded at the least an A-. My classmates thought I overreacted. Touché; their complacency unsettled me. Many of them yielded to whatever their teachers served them and said, "Thank you ". Not me, I didn't neglect to force a, "Fuck you" out of my mouth. I asked for what I deserved —and more. Every facet of my temper advertised: he's inappropriate.

My friendships were no different. The mental and physical effort I exercised was too much work for me: heeding your own voice in a group of young men presents no easy task--you battle not only your insecurities, but more terrifyingly, theirs also. And I always found befriending males somewhat arduous and useless anyway, even until this day. Most males ape each other's behaviors and beliefs like the simians they are. They think I look down on them but if only they ceased to look up at me. But, I know their true intentions: similar to intelligence gathering, males insist on knowing more about you so that they can use their knowledge of you against you. The room to roam about as an undeterred spirit became increasingly restricted around other males, so, I usually found myself crashing against walls meant to keep me in.

One random night, I went out for drinks with my one of the few males I trust, Mike. We would often escape to Benny Burritos, a Mexican restaurant in Greenwich Village, where $4 margaritas drifted us off into a world where idealism was not harassed and we could speak honestly about all the dreams we had, those dreams that most people our age hide within themselves. The restaurant perched itself on the corner with a view of the old world New York City walk up buildings across the street, which had now been turned into fashionable havens for the rich.

That night I presented an idea to him: "I got a way for us to get out of here and make money at the same time--somewhere we can go and just maybe not have to deal with the un-realities of the American work machine." Mike worked excruciating hours at two jobs, so I knew his adventurous side would lead him down an interesting path along with me. I however, had recently lost my job due to New York State budget cuts. But, apart of me ventured to return to an old dream of mine that failed to burn out: the need to just live--to unleash myself from the stakes of the American workplace. Willing to stall my career by spending a few years abroad, I promised myself that I would chance traveling the entire world if I could find a peaceful place where I didn't have to jeopardize my torrid attitude. I thought about working at a job that treated its employees fairly, with respect, and as equals. Ahh, the idealism of youth plays horrible tricks on the mind! Yes, that idealism that most of us caress in our youth then let slip from our grasp as we solidify into mature, responsible adults. I waged on keeping my idealism.

Late February 2012 I boarded a Singapore Airlines flight to Seoul, South Korea. I envisioned a new horizon, new possibilities, and a brand new start. When I arrived, I was greeted with stares of shock and bewilderment. The first week there was no class for the students so I was left to sit at a desk and just stare at my computer screen. When school did start, my co-teacher Jen berated me for not rising at the very moment the school bell rung. It was her expectation that when the school bell rung that I was suppose to line up at the door and wait for her, and walk behind her. It was dejavu.

Most of the Korean teachers suffered from the same commercialism that plagued the United States. My first week there, Jen and the other co-teachers joked about all of the Korean teachers who had some kind of plastic surgery done to their face. "South Korea is known as the plastic surgery capital of Asia," they laughed together. "And we love, love, love shopping." It seemed their whole basis for going to work was solely to consume some sort of cosmetic product. Many Koreans, both male and female, lived at home until they married so their financial responsibilities were limited. The city was over-saturated with all types of markets (clothing, electronics especially) all selling similar products, whereby it made the city look really vivacious; but, it was all a veneer. Every other store sold the same products at the same price--the only thing that was different was the bright flashing lights on the front of each retailer. Little things like this helped me to see how western capitalism had spread its tentacles across the globe along with its penchant for meaningless consumption and competition. Koreans would go to any lengths to show their parity with the United States and other countries like Japan and it was this sense of endless competition that was beginning to overtake their culture as it has done to so many other countries in the west.

The students gave me respite from the other teachers and administrators who decried my presence as a nuisance: one, I was an American; two, I was a black American. I think the former irritated them more than the latter. Just read the headlines. The Guardian printed an article on February 7, 2014, titled "Rejection of Irish teacher highlights South Korean xenophobia," showcasing the issue. After having taught English in Barcelona, Oxford, Abu Dhabi and Seoul, Katie Mulrennan was surprised to receive an email response to her foreign teacher application that stated: "Hello Katie, I am sorry to inform you that my client does not hire Irish people due to the alcoholism [sic] nature of your kind...the best of luck in the future." (htt12)

South Korea hired me to work in the most conservative school- and the teachers, don't get me started on the teachers- they were an obsequious bunch to speak cautiously. At every turn they failed to apprehend their fear seeing me as their career nemesis: they presumed foreign English teachers hijacked their jobs—but, when don't natives think they are entitled to a job? -- As if any employer had an obligation to provide for nationalist sentiment.

Most of the foreign teachers didn't care to really teach so they found it no offense when the Korean co-teacher dragged them along by the collar and propped the foreigner up behind them. It symbolically showed that the citizens of the United States no longer demanded respect. I however, posed a problem. I rebelled: I didn't stand behind my co-teachers like a foreign toy to play with. I jumped right in there, headstrong, and did my job, and unlike many other foreign teachers, I actually churned out a neuron or two. Standing in as the only foreign teacher at my school, I learned a new meaning for the term isolation. As I walked the hallways, both students and teachers spoke ill of me in my face, using any and every xenophobic term they knew to bash the American. "Waygook, waygook," meaning, "foreigner, foreigner," they said as they laughed. Cute the first month, but by month five I wanted to go down to Itaewon, where the US military stationed many soldiers, and organize a blitzkrieg against their asses.

To my dismay, South Korean public schools organized themselves like the North Korean government. The building housed coldness like no other. The students wore puff coats and kept their hoods on in class to protect themselves from the bitter winds. The old dirty brown brick building rested in front of a military area, an area closed off to the public. The school teachers joked about how secretive the area was and guessed at what the South Korean military might be doing back there. The building itself seemed to be a relic of the old world that refused to leave its post. Out front, the students played soccer on hard surfaces, the grass refused to grow in many areas of the city.

The teachers attributed their stiff obedience to the school administration as "cultural norms," and their behavior foreboded a tough year ahead. I understood the meaning of respecting cultural boundaries, however, this surpassed conformity. Korean teachers worked in a state of constant fear. For example, the public school system required the teachers to change schools every number of years in order that they gain experience at different school sites. But anyway with the slightest sense could see that the purpose was to prevent teacher cohesiveness—aka, unions. One way my school roped in teacher's independent thought was to never give them time to meet without the administrations presence. Everyday, the administration expected teachers to eat lunch with the administration in the cafeteria (which, was really the principal's office used also as a cafeteria). And each day the administration looked over the faculty eyeing us with suspicion. Meanwhile, the teachers ate their daily portions of soup and Kim chi while allotting a cursory glance towards the administration to see if their conversations were appropriate enough. Everyday—soup and Kim chi—everyday. Everyday they asked, "Cedric, do you like Kim chi?"-As if they didn't see me spoon-feeding myself like a self-sufficient baby. "Kim chi too hot for waygook," they laughed. At the beginning of the school year I conceded by eating whatever the cafeteria served. My ass burned hotter than the lakes of hell after eating Kim chi. A month into the school year my gastrointestinal system normalized the abuse, and the pain subsided.

Besides that, teachers didn't speak to me at lunch. They expected that I sit and listen to their conversations in Korean as I nod my head, even though some knew English. If I didn't show up to lunch, it became the talk of the school. "Where was Cedric? Is he sick?" I was sick—sick of their shit! At the beginning of the year I followed custom: I waited for everyone to finish their lunch before darting out of the cafeteria to the bathroom. At lunch, no teacher dared stand up to leave before the principle even if their bladders were to suddenly explode--nothing moved them to act before the administration. They rose from the table at the same time, all cleaned their bowls and treys out at the same time, and all walked out of the cafeteria/office like a centralized regime.

By month three, I stopped eating in the lunchroom as a form of protest. My co-teacher, Jen, had it out for me. At the very last minute before each class she would say, "Oh Cedric, I saw your lesson plan, I have questions." When the school bell rang, she jumped up out of her seat and left the office even though she and I were co-teaching the same class. Sometimes we broke out into a full-fledged verbal assault on each other in the office--and at times, in the classroom in front of the students. As a result, the other Korean teachers treated me like I acquired Ebola. She really despised me. The idea of me teaching instead of sitting in the back of the class, or better yet, behind her, disturbed her to the core. Before I knew it, teachers who smiled at me the beginning of the year, now frowned at me and turned the other direction when they saw me. Once again, I lost companionships on account of my refusal to kneel. However, toughness builds character, and it overflowed from my mouth. And so let me say this: couching authoritarianism inside the slogan "cultural norms," fools only the foolish.

Jen's insistence on teaching me a lesson culminated in the usual admonishing letter from the school coordinator, which I've grown accustomed to over the years. One day in December, I received an email from the coordinator of the program:

=========================
12/16/12

From: Jon Pak
To: Cedric Hines

Hi Cedric Hines,

We need to have a talk about your behavior and schoolwork.
Please leave me your contact information or please give me a call
after your classes.

Thank you.

=========================

I've found that at the heart of schooling lays obedience; at the
bottom of the labor market fester obedience; and circumventing
our socialization, obedience. I barely made it out of South Korea
with my head. Sometimes I imagined the immigration sending a
government agent to my apartment in the middle of the night to
boot me out of the country. But, surprisingly I finished the school
year in good standing.

February of 2013, I served my time in South Korea and came
home. As I debarked a Korean Air airliner at San Francisco
International Airport, I grinned with a sense of success. The skies
cleared the path for me, so clear and turquoise; not one cloud
hovered overhead, and not a trace of fog. After a year of teaching
in a country some labeled the iron wall of Asia, in a place that I
think never had seen or conceived of such a vision, I felt as if the
weather provided an omen that I could tackle any complexity life
threw at me. California looked different to me, however. On the
way from the airport, I saw rest stops along the highway closed
due to budget cuts. The cars on the freeway even looked
different, no longer overcrowded with oversized SUVs', but now
hybrids and smaller, thrifty vehicles. More people at the gyms at
2pm, and less traffic during rush hour surprised me. Starbucks
cups now severalized the upper middle-class from the lower
middle-class by the mere presence of a cup logo. Looking out, I
knew any future ambitions swirling in my mind might succumb
to the world's reality if I did not guard against it. Determined, I
reiterated that their reality did not make my reality.

If I could help it, I would spend the rest of my life traveling and immersing myself in other cultures and lifestyles. But, the reality of my situation roped me back into the labor market. Very few people escape the workplace and it's inherently visceral battles: battles with everyone and everything; the employee with the employee; the employee with the manager; the manager with the CEO, etc. The great recession gave no sign of tiring out. It had been this world wind, which carried me away to South Korea in the first place. But, travel bestowed something more revealing in me: a sense of the limitless possibilities available in life, but this feeling lasted only so long before the American reality confronted me once again. Nothing changed since leaving the country; all of my problems sat waiting patiently for my return.

The debates on CNN raged on without end or resolution. I turned the news off and clicked off the job search sites as they upset me. I clicked open my blog, illtidings.com, and wrote an article about Planned Parenthood and their conflicts with conservatives. I hit the keys hard as I typed "FUCKING IDIOTS," then erased it because I know some readers stop listening soon as the do-gooders see a curse word! I saw my country taking steps backwards, walking in the footsteps of our ignorant ancestors, morphing into something altogether horrifically puritanical and I could honestly say, it frightened me. I gazed out the window; peering between the white shutters my mom recently installed in her living room. I daydreamed. I imagined myself becoming this renowned writer who lived from the earnings he received from his book sales. What a dream! Then, another image intruded; I saw myself unwashed and clothed in layers of used clothing I picked up at the salvation army, without any money to feed or house myself.

As I sat in the comforts of my mother's gated community, I realized how accustomed I had become to this lifestyle and the thought of losing it seemed a rational fear. The labor market causes this fear to take hold of people everywhere. The middle-class strived to secure riches to compete with their neighbors: Who drives the biggest car? Who owns the biggest house? Meanwhile the rich dreaded the thought of creeping profits: waking up and going to sleep obsessing over their wealth to the point that their blessings burden them. And the poor shuddered from the chills of the cold world, which had totally locked them out of the financial system. No matter what your socio-economic status, you are pushed and pulled at in every direction, here, there, all over the globe chasing jobs and "opportunities."

However, there's a stark difference between the rich and the working poor. The rich concern themselves only with affording to remain themselves. It's only the working poor that live with desperation to crawl up and over their socio-economic status. The quest for upward mobility left them forever in a tenuous state of potential loss and wished for gain. They all tremble in this arena. But, instead of lions they have each other to devour. If you've ever seen television footage of how these people act on Black Friday every year after Thanksgiving--running and stomping each other to the ground for a discounted item they can actually find online for the same price--then you have a good vision of how they behave at work, at home, at church, at the grocery store, on the subway...

On those days when I let my mind wander I've contemplated the fact that I never agreed, tacitly or explicitly, to any form of economic "social contract": what I'm saying is, I never consented to this economy to wrap me up in its merciless arms. I never agreed to go along with the work system. If I was given a way out, I would take it and run so far away and with so much speed. If we go along with the system, it strangles us and convinces us this is for our own good (i.e., hard work)—if we oppose it, it just strangles us (e.g. homelessness, hunger). Nobody has ever written such a thing as an economic social contract, and no cause or justification ever given nor any argument of why I benefited enough to join this ulcer of modernity. Even if a contract did appear, I would tear it to pieces. For, we often assume that an activity performed in exchange for payment constitutes free labor; however, free labor insinuates a freewill! But, some of our most popular philosophers have already denounced and proven "free will" to be a figment of the human imagination. For, there is no free will with threats of harm. And in the workplace free will could not exist because that would imply that we were not impeded by the threat of homelessness, hunger, and poverty. To add, most of us never had a choice. Warned from birth we hide under the slogan: work or starve. Unlucky enough not to have lived before the Homestead Acts--a period which today's elite and wealthy owe many of their grandfathered properties--we owned no land to till, no lands to feed ourselves, nothing to trade, nothing to clothe ourselves, nothing to help ourselves, except the wear and tear of our own bodies.

Doesn't this situation sound familiar? Once upon a time slavery too presided as the norm. Then, as a thief in the night, came the wage laborer and uprooted slave labor. Yet, the goals and side-effects remain the same. The only difference today is that instead of one race, all races are now wrapped up into a global slavery like none other before it. Now "liberated" from the chains of American slavery, the time clock and the early morning sacrifice to misery vindicate us. Few question the legitimacy of this regime, but then again few questioned the justice of slavery in its first hundred years. Let it be known from this moment that forced labor or that which fools call "gainful employment," happened against our will, and we have lost ever since. Don't talk to me about "at will employment."

We should redefine at will employment as the ability to feed, clothe, and house oneself without the burden of labor. One should regain a choice whether to make extra income beyond subsistence, which calls for our governments to stop manufacturing scarcity. And don't give me that hoopla about the Tragedy of the Commons.

Many of nights, I imagined sitting in my bedroom, playing oldies such as Aretha Franklin's Master of Eyes, Janet Jackson's New Agenda, Donny Hathaway's Little Ghetto Boy and Fleetwood Mac's Silver Spring's on repeat, while papers fluttered around the room cover every inch of the wood floor, and quotes blanketing the walls, as I sit, writing, without fear of starvation or homelessness. I don't know of anyone in my personal life that has ever escaped this system and its cycles of poverty: the cycle of at will employment. But, "Time is money," they say, and that's all a dream in my head.

CHAPTER 2: Back to Reality

Thirty minutes into my research, my best friend Latoya called. I reached for my Iphone, "Wussup?" She chuckled, "Hey friend." But, I could discern from the forced laughter that she brought something else to the conversation besides good tidings. We went through the usual, "How are you doing," but it didn't take long to get to the intended purpose of the call.

"You know," she said, elongating the letters, "ow," "that damn job is cutting my hours." A tinge of anxiety shook me, thinking what the end of her story might entail. A brief moment of silence sat heavily between us, as we both knew the consequences of such an event. Latoya recently gave birth to her first child so this was the last piece of news she needed. "They're just doing this so they can pocket more money," her voice stiffened. " They're installing some automated system that will cheaply do my job. I got to get out of here quick man." She sounded determined. But, even while trying to empathize with her situation I couldn't help think of my own. While dreaming of becoming a writer, the realness of both of our situations caused me to reconsider my future dreams. My dreams would remain parked if I didn't do something about it, but who has the time? If people with more experience, more education, and more wealth worried about the current state of the job market, what made me exempt from this tide of fear? But I shook that doubt for I knew that employers win if you bow to helplessness. Seeing Latoya in this position, and standing incapable of helping her, tugged at me the most. It's what tugs at us all; we want to see our brothers, sisters, cousins, and best friends succeed. Nevertheless, when you watch a situation like this and do nothing about it, you unknowingly feed into the system. You become a slave voyeur, and you thank the heavens that it's not happening to you. However, don't think for a moment it will not come knocking at your door at some point. Employers win because employees lose—and because employees see themselves as losers unless they succeed at the game dictated by the employer.

As Latoya continued to explain her situation I drifted off into my own world with its separate set of problems--all different, yet, all the same. As employees, we remained subjected to the threat of displacement. In practice, this fear tactic aimed to keep workers subordinate and obedient. Restructuring reuses an old tactic used by employers to hold power over employees. I once heard the word "restructuring" in a job interview, as a young man, and more naïve about how power operated. After I was hired and the months drifted by, I came to understand my role within the organization. The CEO changed the chain of command for my position. My position would now report to both, the director and the CEO, and sometimes the director didn't know what went on between me and the CEO, thereby circumventing her authority. The purpose: to maintain division between me and my director so as not to counter the power of the CEO. And this was a non-profit organization!

If employers really wanted to reorganize their departments differently, for organizations sake, they would rearrange their employees like a network instead of operating like the Gestapo. That entailed destroying the power arrangement—i.e. the sole reason for work. The idealistic side of me wanted to think that our future looked forward in angst and rage to the day when those above and below will share in the same luxuries, and work together to fulfill common goals, goals that might change the world at last. Now this would be restructuring! A company parallels a truly reorganized company when you can scarcely tell the difference between a supervisor and his subordinates. Eventually, superiority fades away with it. Nevertheless, equality conforms to the values of those from below, not above. Therefore, it will never have a place in the workforce. Damnit! Al Quaida restructured itself in a more modern way, more so than most of the top ranking corporations.

The existing state of affairs--the great recession -- was turning into something altogether excessive. In recessions before the Republican Party, in all its mendacity, hadn't gone to such great lengths to prevent its own country from getting back on its feet. But for some reason, they hated Barack Obama even more? From the famous yells, "you lie," hurdled at Obama by GOP Rep. Joe Wilson to the also famous finger-pointing incident where Arizona Governor Jan Brewer berated Obama in front of the media. We saw the Republican Party's real face. And it was red and angry. Hmm, I wonder why? I despise the conversation in this nation—or lack of conversation -- which dances and parades around the topic at the core of our ancient and current situation. I hate that we can't speak its name in a supposedly post-

r_____ America. Anyone who speaks of r_____, the
conservatives condemn as delusional. Liberals are no better.
They have all sorts of answers and conclusions for our current
predicament: Bush handed Obama this country in a declining
position in world affairs; globalization is the devil; all the wars
we have waged have helped to squander our moral high ground
-- and GDP; the right and left wing can't get along, etc. Huh!
Although the recession started before Obama's administration, it
slipped into the Great Recession because of his black skin! There,
I said it. Our profiled national conversation on race stands biased
against having an open discussion. Any other justification
proposed suffers from a lack of honesty, credibility, and
seriousness. Our country doesn't know how to treat black men
any differently--its established protocol. The reason we can't
speak openly and honestly about r_____ is because we sweep
r_____ under the rug. Meanwhile, the plight of Black men
remains ignored and looked over—the government doesn't see
us, it sees the past. It longs for those predictable days when it
could do with us whatever it pleased; now, it's silenced beyond its
own belief and harbors such rage for us that it can't even
pronounce our names correctly. (E.g., they pronounce Obama as
Osama; they pronounced 2pac Shakur as 2-pack Shakur.)
Blaming Obama surfaced as the right's justification for never
voting any blacks, women, or any minority for that matter, into
office again. Minorities just want to exist in peace. Yet, we
remain victims and setbacks: when they see us marching up the
hill in all our exceptional glory they want to shoot us down.
Nevertheless, this merits no new study. For the longest,
minorities in America have created our own worlds outside the
majorities' opinion of us; we walk through and past them without
judging or giving credibility to their dislike of us and their self-
hatred. No more will we tolerate their slogan: "in statu quo res
erant ante bellum." The work of the minority warrants
overcoming the status quo of the majority at all and any cost.

The strong undercurrents of racism during Obama's
administration justify the argument that r_____ is part and
parcel of the American dream. "Race... is a much more recent
idea, tied up with the founding of the U.S [htt1]." It follows
upward mobility, up and over the colored peoples of America. It's
as if, "Life should be better and fuller," for everyone except
darker complexions. All men are created equal? When? Equality
has never, and never will exist in America or any other land on

earth. The same people who believe in the "second coming" fabricate stories of equality. The lower classes invented this term out of thin, and polluted air to ameliorate their existence. While they wait for equality, I'll take my piece of heaven now!

If you listen to the right, Obama's proletarian policies sank the country into a dark hole. I would go down as remiss not to mention the fact that our country lives by the doctrine of Laissez Faire, not Liberté, égalité, fraternité. However, let's also not forget that Abraham Lincoln's policies led towards a United States of America and settled in our national psyche as intrinsically proletarian. His policies indirectly created, what, most left-wingers, and all right wingers call, the greatest nation on earth. So, as far as I'm concerned, both left and right-wingers drink from the same filthy pond.

I think what bothered me the most about South Koreans was their people pleasing tendencies. Not so much because I cared about the politics of their nation—because, I truly didn't! —But, people like that make it difficult for people like myself to find breathing room on this earth. Am I projecting? Maybe. A wave of complacency overtook America in such a short amount of time between 2001 and 2014. "The land of the free." The launch of the War on Terror—with its goalless ends and borderless desires—easily persuaded American citizens to step on the American constitution and turn their backs on the truth. Everywhere they looked, danger; the world became a scary place after September 11th, 2001. And what did they do? They adhered to the advice of greedy politicians who claimed to protect them if they would only hand over a few of their rights. Lo and behold, we lucked out to get the Patriot Act. The Patriot Act became the War on Terror; the War on Terror mutated into fear at home; fear at home changed into a justification for drones abroad; drones succeeded so well overseas, our loving and protecting government bought some to watch over us here at home. Witnessing what fear can do to simple-minded folks vexed me. How do you succeed in a world that deliberately inconveniences you, making you feel it seem as if life is closing in on you? How much longer would humanity grovel on the ground before it realized it had the power to walk? My future peered out over the horizon with these questions in mind.

My conversation with Latoya turned to silence as we both

contemplated the fact that we had spoke about this topic numerous times since we entered the labor force but we could never come together to reach a satisfying conclusion, which would benefit the both of us. To ease the unsatisfactory reality, we turned the conversation in an easier direction then hung up.

Daydreaming on the couch I remembered an advertisement I saw for a massive hiring frenzy in New York City. The New York City Teaching Fellows were conducting a search for educated people without professional teaching experience in the United States. Their reasoning was that that they wanted to expand New York City student's exposure to professionals from different educational backgrounds. It suited me perfectly since I didn't have a teacher's license, but did enjoy teaching overseas; not to mention I had planned to return to NYC within the next month and it would be nice for once to return with the immediate possibility of work--and hence, a paycheck. I put my blog's tab to the far side as I dragged the Teaching Fellows tab to the front. I clicked on their websites link and researched the organization and the job. I clicked apply.

CHAPTER 3: New York Teaching Fellows-"You're Cheap Labor"

Up until this point, I equated leaping from job to job as natural. What was always unnatural to me, however, was spending the rest of my life working for someone else.

After returning to New York City from California, I immediately embarked on an adventure. I put in an application for the New York City Teaching Fellows alternate certification-teaching program. My interview took place on March 13, 2013. They called it an interview but when potential fellows arrived they labeled it an information session; those still interested in continuing the process went online and chose a time-slot right after the information session. I chose March 19, 2013, at M460 Washington Irving High School in Manhattan. I lucked out on one of the last interview dates available as hiring season started four months earlier. I received an email notification April 4, 2013, stating: "Congratulations! On behalf of the New York City Department of Education, I am pleased to inform you that you have been accepted to the NYC Teaching Fellows June 2013 program. You have been accepted to train to teach Special Education Your acceptance to the Fellowship recognizes your achievements to date, your demonstrated teaching potential, and your commitment to the children of New York City."

On June 17, 2013, Cohort 24 Fellows poured in by the hundreds into the 2013 welcoming ceremony held at Baruch College on 23rd Street and Lexington Ave. The line stretched around the block, littered with poor souls now saved by the prospects of employment. Inside, the first speaker spoke from a prepared speech announcing that they picked two hundred fellows out of eleven hundred applicants. We lucked out.

The Fellows program rounded out to two sections: The Fellows Training program (which last one summer) and the University assignment -- where the Fellow takes classes to obtain their Masters of Science in Teaching in two and a half years. The next day all of the District 75 Special Education Fellows met at their pre-destined University. They enrolled me at Pace University, and District 75 (D75) served as my potential employment district: D75 handled all the city's severely disabled students. I chose this program as I liked a challenge, and worked with disabled populations previously.

On July 1, 2013, the University held a Teaching Fellows General Meeting to introduce Fellows to the academic environment of Pace University and its rules and regulations. Seats lined the room forming a half-circle facing the front, where an insignia of Pace University hung next to a large smart board screen. On the side, they made refreshments available for everyone to take. In the back, two rectangular tables faced each other on each side of the entrance. Here, the fellows signed in and picked up informational packets. The room looked beyond orderly everything and everyone in place. All the fellows were trafficketing to their seats anticipating what surprises awaited them.

The Fellows Program wanted the meeting to appear as if their recruits were the prized possessions to be sold to the highest bidder. They required Fellows to present themselves in clothes that gave off the message that these employees will do any and everything, even change their outward appearance, to be sold to principles and vice principles. Not only was the physical appearance of the Fellows important, but also their mental capacity. Employers, especially public employers, do not prize individuality and those who retain a sense of themselves. The most intelligent teachers were not wanted--those who could obey the most, however, appealed more to their taste. The main reason the Teaching Fellows do not recruit Teachers with traditional educational training is that teachers who are certified are knowledgeable about what they should and should not be doing; they can tell the difference between what's best for student achievement and what's best for administrative achievement (financial gain). Traditional teachers would undermine the system of chattelhood. Traditional teachers are more likely to quit and bail out on their duties once they see that they were hired to be manipulated by corrupt administrations.

One speaker that day laid the ground rules of the game we were to play. She established in the most rudimentary manner that we as Fellows stood as not examples of achievement, but the lowest common denominator. Her name was Jackie Keane and she bagged the title, principle, at a District 75 school, M138; the school has multiple sites found throughout Manhattan and the Bronx. Keane, a somewhat elder-ish looking rotund white lady mounted the podium. A scene from Peewee's Big Adventure passed through my mind: "Here comes large Marge." With her husky voice, white Golden Girls hair (think Betty White without the makeup and comic relief, better yet, without all the good qualities), and a wobble—resulting from her weight and age--she approached the podium to address all the Fellows. As she tried to gasp for breath looking out over the crowd of potential Yes-men and Yes-women, she panted the following: "Welcome. You all are desired by Principle's because, well, you're cheap labor," she smiled. Then she hinted at how easy principles could mold us, then, before she got too ahead of herself, she contested the statement by pretending to play a joke on us. A disconnect between our realities and her reality widened even further. The crowd chuckled in a way reminiscent of what I had read about in college--the way in which Soviets felt compelled to applaud whenever dictator Joseph Stalin uttered one syllable and how nobody wanted to sit down first or stop clapping first. The entire spectacle amounted to the beginning of a calculated indoctrination into the world of Public Education in New York City: an autocratic regime of power salivating megalomaniacs who demanded nothing less than the steepest regard for their authority!

I oscillated in my seat to determine who responded negatively or positively to that woman's honky-tonk statement; I kept my opinion to myself. Excepting me and a few not paying attention, the fellows swayed to a unanimous positive. Attempting to hide my true emotions I maintained a half-smirk as anything less in the eyes of the Fellows equated to an unthankful demeanor and a display of ungratefulness for this blessed position. As I would soon discover, any signs of disapproval or even worse the serious violation of having an opinion, neither the Fellows nor the Department of Education (DOE) would tolerate. My eyes bounced from the floor to the podium in a linear direction as I thought of all the things I could and should do besides sitting here and pouring my life away listening to a bunch of old bureaucratic bats orally gyrate back and forth about how long they worked for the DOE. Only item missing was a wet towel!

I doubled over, dying a prolonged death, listening to her fustian announcements as she addressed a room filled with passionate fellows with such carelessness. Each word she spoke created a further divide between her and the rest of us. Apart of me wanted to blurt out: you're already taking eight hours of my life, which I will never get back, what else do you want, my blood? -- Sit yo old-decrepit ass down! But calming myself, I resolved to quell that part of Cedric. I needed to maintain a sense of composure. But, each moment that passed also took with it a little of my dignity. But, then again, every day that I walked out of my apartment on 135th street, I saw people sitting on the stoops of their apartment complexes and then I would see these same individuals sitting on the stoop when I came home from work, tired and worn out. Not all of them looked miserable. Some even looked content living without working and they reminded me of untarnished canvasses. They had probably never known what it meant to go to work everyday and be ridiculed by wage labor. If welfare was okay for them, could it possibly content me? But then you'll have those who say that people on welfare are lazy but as I thought over their situation and mine, I started to see that they were smart! Why run your life to the ground working for some slave machine when you could sit at home and enjoy your life? The poor are no different than the rich--both know the meaning of leisure. It was only the working poor, in all their morals and dignity that fought to stay in a game that was rigged against them.

I could see Keane peering out at the crowd calculating how many she could hire for the least buck, and in exchange, get rid of tenured teachers. My spirit cracked into pieces, pieces itemized and sold the lowest bidder. I knew this haranguing wouldn't last too much longer I'm sure they didn't want to beat us so bad we'd cling to the ropes because they hired us for a reason--to work. In their mercy, they knew we needed a minimal amount of self-respect to raise ourselves up in the morning to, once again, anxiously watch our mortality slip from us.

I cashed out. I started to daydream, or hallucinate possibly, about the places that called out for me—Greece, Brazil, Spain. I heard enough; not just of this overgrown stem of bureaucracy standing before me, but of the whole matter. Why did I have to be here? Why couldn't I be rich? What could I do--or would I have to do -- to become rich? Her words blazed me into ashes, and then I came to my senses. I deposited my soul here for a paycheck. Wait, wait, wait—is that what life's about? If it is, we need to reposition the respect given to the process of garnering a paycheck. All we need to do is look through the lenses of history and mankind's dehumanization of other human beings to see that a paycheck is no reward or anything to brag about. Think about what we do for a paycheck! We laugh and smile for eight hours a day while our personal lives calcify into disrepair, and our hearts break. We agree to subjects and topics that we don't agree with. We lose. We lose our voice and our ability to speak up. We forget our first-born instincts. Daily, employers inundate us with lies and fabrication of lies to the point that we don't remember where we came in or how to get out. I can't find one employee who still holds the dignity they once held onto as a child. "Out of the mouths of babes." Employees bury these gems deep inside of themselves when they enter the work force hoping senselessly that a raise or promotion might be enough to dig that gem from the deep recesses of their creative imaginations.

The way I see it, my life imparted me a blank paycheck and I made it out to The Teaching Fellows/New York City Department of Education. Let's face it; all we ever get from employers is our life and that was free to begin with. We received nothing else--no surplus income, no surplus living, nothing else. A realization surfaced: as free people we could have taken care of our ourselves on our own. Except that, "Brilliant," capitalist maliciously thought to hoard land and resources for their own profit—and jokingly they required us to ask for permission to use this same land by paying rent! What a joke! If you think about it, civilized society is the result of nothing other than the rot of thieving and conniving individuals. And as the rest of us declare faith as our last hope--if we have it— who can tell me the worth of that?

Take your faith and give me ignorance! Ignorance trails bliss. For when one lifts the veil from over the eyes of the employee, and they find that their paycheck was merely a joke they soon discover their sin--losing that spitefulness to spit in the face of servitude. And the wages of sin: wage slavery. Spending my life working for someone else violates human nature. Employment masks no minor sin; its evils brought mortal consequences for us all leading to nothing but emptiness and darkness. The reason we have SSI serves as a safety net to catch the employee after his life of servitude abandons him to sickness and death.

When the employee first entered the labor market, he worked for his pay--the level of work measured out to the payment of wages.

Then came the time clock. Time changed everything. Employers thought to themselves how could we squeeze the people for more work, thereby increasing our profits? Yes! We can measure their pay by time instead of labor intensity. From that time on, time measured the burden of men on a scale of hours. For instance, at the Teaching Fellows the program ran a slavishly long day from 8am to 6pm, but the work extended into the night hours also without pay. The time clock stands as one of the most hideous inventions of all time. Time is money and that's all it is.

To keep from falling prey to the speaker's protracted belittlement of the crowd, I leaned back to hear two female Fellows quietly discussing their career endeavors. Each of them appeared to be native New Yorkers based on their accents--as opposed to the many Fellows who were hired from out of state. The second, a well put together Latina, with apparent tattoos which she half-heartedly attempted to cover with a scarf that hung loosely on her neck, took on a very confident, assured demeanor. It was as if she waited for this job for a lifetime. The other woman, a 50ish looking Jewish woman from Brooklyn, who looked like she might have lost herself at Woodstock, presented herself as someone who never gave up on the idealism of the 70's.

As the Latina inexpensively laid out her past employment, the Jewish lady cut her short and stated," Well you know this serves as a process for me; I already have a job lined up for me once I finish the program in August, so I'm not too concerned about the job opportunities available." The Latina extended her silence a notch passed the usual waiting period, then in a way signaling that the Jewish lady truncated her thought she continued, "Yea, so, I've been helping out in the schools for many years now assisting teachers and staff to better serve at risk youth in the city's schools." The Jewish lady, facing forward, nodded in approval and the conversation collapsed for a moment.

I thought to myself this really was a rat race.

Competition on the job reminds me of the fugitive who runs away and is ratted out by his own people. Working people usually end up defeating themselves. I can't stand people like this; I reject them from my memory if I can, if only owed to their dejected disposition. To them, winning any victory betrayed the rebuke of deception, malevolence, and mendacity. You know them by the dirt on the bottom of their souls. These self-hating persons conquer their own pride first even if they believe they have conquered their opponent. Their extreme and prejudiced dislike of themselves cause them to remain in the closet they so wish to come out of. They lie and wait in dark corners for you to make the slightest mistake so they can project and put on display their own fears of retribution--of which they fully deserve. Who hasn't come across these queers? Low self-esteem taps the least of the worker's concerns. People like this maintain the psychiatry profession. We need a new way of thinking about victory: winning wins when you can push yourself past yourself; when you compel even the atoms and cells within you to go in a desired direction. Going along with the "process" means that you reflect only an outgrowth of a larger organism. A winner self-replicates, self-creates, and self-contains. An organ that commands wins -- anything else plays on the term. And believe me, they prevail at pretending to grasp the heart of one of us self-contained ones, but you can tell them by their fruit: the smiles that never breach the line of sincerity; the handshakes, which always hang like their pride.

You have won when your self-doubt clasp its hands before your desire, when you stop asking so many questions, and for once, answer some. Men and women like these two always think they have achieved something great when they defeat another coworker; whole societies build themselves on this idea. We self-contained ones usually fall victim to these types because of such ignorance, but do we not have a ball while we dance here on earth? Interpersonal relationships always succumb to another's half-empty selves even those half-full want to suck you dry to complete themselves. Yet, men like Jesus, Karl Marx, and Martin Luther King, incited fear in entire societies, not by force, but by overcoming themselves.

The conversation picked up again in a deliberate manner as to avoid the awkwardness that just reared its ugly face. "So," the Jewish lady said, "this mayor is really going to be a pain in our ass," referring to then Mayor Bloomberg. The Latina smiled in agreement. "Teachers and the Union can't do anything to change the system in this city, it's built to make sure that poor students get the least, if even that. The best we can do is ensure we don't lose our jobs, and then I guess we can teach when there is time to do so," the Jewish lady said looking for an applause. "I've heard horror stories about these schools and the administrators, I have friends throughout the public school system, I know," she uttered in her Brooklyn accent. "The day is coming soon when I won't have to work. My husband makes a good enough salary, ya know, soon I'll break free from this," she pointed to the podium where Jackie Keane was still rambling on, and then at the crowd. The Latina lady shook her shoulders in laughter to give her new friend the assurance she sought.

"But yea, this Mayor is a piece of shit," the Jewish lady felt compelled to say to bridge the gap in the conversation. Her complaints about Mayor Bloomberg ran a long list and for the most part were true. I knew some of the facts about Mayor Bloomberg from basic research. Just to name a few.

* First, he took control of the city's schools in 2002 under the policy of Mayoral Control, where he virtually stripped the school boards--run by officials elected by the community--and replaced their power with his private board, the Panel for Educational Policy, a non-elected, but, selected, panel of individuals the Mayor believed suitable to decide the fate of all New York City students

* His insistence on a failed "Children First" policy--New York City's version of No Child Left behind

* Emphasis on "high stakes" testing based on accountability for students, teachers, and administrators, but mostly for teachers seeing as many on the left came to believe, the Mayor hated teachers

* The imposition of school grades, based on an A-F system similar to the city's rating of restaurants--a system in which the Mayor stigmatized schools for not meeting inflated standards set by the city, thereby subjecting these same schools to the Mayor's next, and signature, policy

* Closing schools "not performing" to standards, many of which happened to culminated in poor neighborhoods leaving families with no choices in their community; in this way the Mayor could put pressure on the city's parents to rally for charter schools, of which the Mayor stood as the biggest proponent. Charter schools opened placements inside city buildings alongside public schools

in which the stark differences in economic inequality flourish to this day in order to persuade parents to come over to the Charter school side and leave public schools in the dust (when the mayor closed schools and combined schools into single building, sometimes six schools might shutter in one building, sharing building space and sometimes the same floor)

* A last piece of evidence rested in the decline in tenure granted to teachers who served three years probation. Add to that, belittling and degrading the United Federation of Teachers in New York City

* The Mayor steadfastly stood behind the Leadership Academies; a fast track program where those wishing to change city schools (imposing their political views), could become principles in New York City schools. The Leadership Academy bred a new type of principal, the "CEO principle," those more concerned about the bottom line and administrative savings, than the fate of students (think Mayor Bloomberg in tacky business casual)

* In order to meet the new standards imposed on the schools when the Mayor took office, the city scrambled to hire teachers to fulfill these obligations but could not make ends meet. Not surprisingly, to the rescue, arrived the New York City Teaching Fellows. That's all it took. Create a demand impossible to fulfill, and then bring in "outside" contractors to fulfill the obligations, which have in mind to push a new "urban revitalization" of New York City public schools

Michael Bloomberg commenced an anti-literacy campaign on teachers: He bridged the close association he believed existed between literate teachers, knowledgeable of their rights, and teachers resistant to injustice, inequality, and political back scratching; an association that could not continue under his watch. Thereby, he set a pre-condition to disincentive certain teachers from working--in particular, those who spoke out and those with certain political and educational philosophies that didn't align with his master plan.

The consequences devastated the school system: Disenfranchised teachers are disenchanted teachers! When you continue to bureaucratize and "modernize" schools for the worse, the enigmatic character of teaching vanishes. To Bloomberg, the crude, sterile, scientific approach to teaching signaled a twist in the right direction. Others might have just called it twisted. He saw increased testing and non-political boards making political decisions as progress.

Teachers felt that he stripped teaching of all its magic. Lets put it like this: Improving educational outcomes starts with empowering teachers with more training! -- And giving them a set of tools of which to choose from, NOT, forcing them to choose specific tools and force them to use the same tools day in and day out; not forcing them to sink or swim. Increasing the strength of the spirit of the teacher, that's improvement--at the current state there's nowhere to go but up. School wide achievement--or educational outcomes--improve as teacher satisfaction improves. This isn't quantum physics here--or for the Department of Education--reading, writing, and arithmetic.

The Mayor, during his reign of terror, thought improving educational outcomes equated to beheading the dignity and pride of teachers system wide. Obviously, some principles, such as Keane, held the same twisted beliefs. She wanted to hire the least knowledgeable teachers to bend and mold them to her backwards design. I entered this system in the summer of 2012. I soon rediscovered something I knew from an early age. That lurking about in our existence here in the developed world, we have managed to dehumanize and belittle the human experience down to an equation! Our human worth equals a paycheck and how much funding we can crank out for others. And in this moment, I realized the extent of boot licking I would have to do to survive here.

Collecting my thoughts, I looked around at the New York City Teaching Fellows associates. A common denominator annunciated something about the whole system. Almost, if not all, the representatives were white women. Not only this, they appeared to be--based on fashion and language accent--not even New York white women. In the months to come I would also visit the fellows office where the same demographic totally dominated. As one walks through 65 Court Street in Brooklyn passed all of the diverse members of the DOE and arrives at the Teaching Fellows floor, the racial makeup makes a noticeable turn that not even Stevie Wonder could miss. It seemed like a great migration from Idaho, or Wyoming occurred while we slept and placed them here in New York City to make change. Specifically, to displace the old teachers who, supposedly, failed at their jobs. So, in comes Middle American white women to the rescue to arrange the improvement of a school system dominated by children of color. I suppose teachers of color aren't exempt from urban revitalization either?

As Jackie Keane finally wrapped up her talk with the new initiates, she commented, "Always remember, children first, the children always come first."

CHAPTER 4: New York Teaching Fellows -Behavior Modification

My faith in the school system cracked before the program even started. The blow from the General Meeting on July 1st sent my mind racing in a hundred different directions. But in the end I knew I needed a job. I lingered in bed the next morning at 5:30am staring at the ceiling. Fifteen minutes passed before I encouraged my muscles to contract and move me to the shower and wash the morning's reluctance off. There's something about a shower, no matter how down I'm feeling in the morning that does more than to awaken me from a short slumber. The shower springs me over the point of no return: I know if I can make it to the shower, the rest of the day splinters. I felt my knee snap into place as I raised myself up. The floor told on me as I stumbled to the bathroom, squeaking along the way. I made it to the shower where the problems I anticipated minutes earlier atrophied. Many of my days would begin this way throughout the summer.

I arrived at Pace University before 8am. The program stressed punctuation like any other professional program: Fellows allowed you three tardies--that included one-minute tardiness--before they expelled you from the program. Towards the end of the summer, half of the Fellows, including myself would receive emails warning us that we had received two tardies and if we incurred one more, would be released from the program--even if it was the last day of training. Let's just say they intended on breaking us from bad habits and our curfew was a serious component of breaking us.

Coaches decorated the classrooms with posters that broadcast the slogans from the Teach Like a Champion Text. Looking to my right or left or behind you couldn't miss the messages of Teach Like a Champion. Their biggest fear was that teachers might learn to draft their own thoughts about how to teach students or maybe worse, they might teach their students to think for themselves?

My class numbered about thirty something fellows. In the mornings we had one summer school class, from 8am-4pm then after that we attended our Fellows training, which focused on teaching Special Education. That lasted from 4pm-630pm. The days extended out into the evening. They regimented us. The days were backbreaking; try sitting down for ten hours a day listening to instructors and coaches. This schedule stretched on for two weeks before the schedule changed, and our teacher assignments distributed. We paired with a summer school teacher to teach children in our age groups, lasting from 8am-12pm. We always ended the day at 630pm, no sooner, and possibly later.

The Fellows program partnered with different Universities in New York City. When Fellows registered for the Fellows Program, the Fellow was automatically enrolled in a University program. To many this might sound like a win-win deal for everyone involved. But who benefits more? Well let's see, the Fellow gets a piece of paper at the end of two and a half years that says he has been educated in the field of teaching. Okay. But, to pay the cost of going to get a Masters degree under the Fellows program (which I must say, is highly discounted)--in order to teach, seems somewhat fuzzy to me. How much can a teacher possibly make in their first year? Between 45-51k. And how much money does the Fellows Program and the University make by enrolling Fellows? And how much do the students benefit? Can anyone calculate that? But, this partnership is supposedly for the children. Anyway....

In the afternoon the Fellows training coach marched in each day and instructed us to watch videos from our Teach Like a Champion textbook. The book focused on common sense topics like: Setting high academic expectations; planning that ensures academic achievement; structuring and delivering your lesson; engaging students in your lesson; creating a strong classroom culture; setting and maintaining high behavioral expectations; building character and trust; improving your pacing; and challenging students to think critically.

The program based itself off the workbook, but the class itself focused on nothing much else but behavioral correction. Actually, all of the classroom videos showed teachers getting students to behave "appropriately." "You can't teach until you get their behaviors in check," the coaches rattled as slogans. I wasn't sure if the videos and posters acted as supports to assist me in keeping my students "in line" or to keep me in "in line." Teach Like a Champion incited my acid reflux. I sat there with each passing day eyebrows drown down like the shades on a window wondering what type of student population we wanted to mold. What I did know was that the Fellows established complete control over our learning, our environment, our time, and our access to families and friends (we worked from sun up to sun down).

In every video, students of color moving, talking, and responding "appropriately" hypnotized me. They were trained to turn both of their legs outside of their desk area at the same time; sit down at the same time; rise at the same time; raise their hands at the same time; fold their hands in the same manner; speak in the right tone of voice; when and when not to speak... Some may ask, well what's wrong with that? -And if you have to ask that question, then you are not the audience I'm writing to. Through repetition, coaches indoctrinated fellows into the suggested behavior they wanted to see in public school students and teachers. Each day that I viewed the videos I was taken back to South Korea. It shocked me to see such behaviors--behaviors reminiscent of videos that showed Nazification of German youth during the Third Reich. And who's to blame? -The parents of course. It's because of the parents in the minds of the system-- their parents failed them. In the eyes of the city and state the parents were degenerates for not providing the students with a "proper" upbringing, but they never care to consider the effects that education inflicts on the family. It's education that wrongs us: education prevents the masses from coming together (e.g. it's education that teaches them morality, but it's also their moralities that pit them against each other. Without moralities, humanity would function the way it was supposed to. Morality establishes our basis for all wars and gripes. But I digress again). Because education prevents them from coming together, it makes it easier for those in power (i.e. the school administrators) to take a proper education from many and give it to some. A proper education would teach a stringent form of selfishness; however, only a few learn this on account of the class war. It's selfishness that educates the rich and wealthy--and it's altruism that educates the working classes. At bottom, I knew most of my future students would be poor and of a multi-ethnic background. Underpinning this alternate-teaching program laid a politically and socially ordained form of eugenics.

Squirming in my seat, I realized how solidly behavior modification ideology formed the foundation of thought at the

Fellows and how much they controlled communication. Short term planning in terms of behavior modification (i.e. addressing behavior as it occurs) sufficed no longer; now, public school officials learned that in order to enforce long term behavioral corrections they needed to plan in advance how and when to address behaviors that might become troublesome for the school system, and as the school system so too the justice system (birds of the same feather, equally faulty and unjust). The children in the videos took in this new "learning" and responded to a new language. The language of containment! It's too much trouble to have to constantly correct a child that looks hell bent on being an individual; it's of the utmost importance to break their minds. In doing this children in urban areas become easier to manipulate for their education is not one of knowledge and wisdom, but one preparing them for an entire lifetime of obedience. The school system operates as a breeding ground for employers in order that they have an everlasting pool of obedient mules to choose from. Programmed to believe it a natural progression (i.e., from school to work), we don't question the utter flippancy of education today (i.e., a truly educated individual shouldn't have to continually update his skills by returning to college or certification programs to stay up to speed with the economy. should he?). The school and work system go hand in hand to create the illusion that society is progressing towards something worthwhile. In reality, we are running on a wheel within a cage going in circles. Those in positions of power put out little snacks for the working class to strive towards, then when too many people begin to succeed at grabbing the snack, the game is changed. A crisis arises. Talk about a new world order! What would happen if the people stopped running? Behavior modification, or better yet, "breaking" students, dazzles as the new vision of public education in New York City. The desired result was fixing the urban problem--they often call it "urban restructuring" when referring to fixing violence in inner city communities, but the same tactics orbit around the schools to get the students under control by containing them in psychological ghettos. Here, the goals and visions limit the students; they often sound the same: "when I grow up I want to be.... (Fill in any job you can think of that adds no value to that person's existence on this earth nor leaves a footprint that they ever existed.) Their dreams are limited and circumscribed by barriers created by their surroundings. For example, the increasing police presence in schools. When students drag their beaten souls into this institution, when the police demand a dark presence in your community to hold you in or to keep you out, when you witness the humiliation and belittlement of your peers--you endeavor to reach goals, which once, were limitless, and are now finite and defined. The defining purpose of law enforcement is societal behavior modification, which impairs you by reining you in along with your dreams.

And so we find that an obedient student cultivates an educated student! How so? Knowledge, skills, and habits of students transfer from one generation to the next through teaching, training, and research of their environment. They learn to fear authority from the law enforcement in their community, to the teacher in the classroom--every encounter with the law becomes a negative occurrence linking interaction with public officials with intimidation and fear. Every interaction trains students in a subtle, indirect behavior lesson. The problem student is one who hasn't quite given up on the spark burning within him, he still disbelieves in the "rules of the game." The school has not yet succeeded in causing the student to re-evaluate the central aspects of his existence--the disobedient student still knows he has a choice and that the world is not flat. Through punishment and reward, obedience breeds a reward, and disobedience breeds a punishment. An educated student learns well what he should say and do at all times. In many of the videos, the teachers stressed that there was either a right or wrong answering without asking the student how he or she came to their conclusions; rarely did I see the teachers in the video bring out the thinking of the student or question their thinking process. As time lines up in a predictable manner his behavior forms apart of his second nature; he stops questioning the world or his surroundings introspectively or holding these questions to the test of logic and human nature. If the school (justice system) succeeds, we will see a change in the student. He then resurfaces from his transformation as the good student that laughs and mocks the student with an alternative, new, enlightening view of the world: and here lies the birth of the basic man and woman (i.e. homophobes, racist, do-gooders, people who laugh at those who are different, genderphiles, people who see an outfit on a mannequin—at a department store of all places—and wear the outfit just like the mannequin, friends who don't invite you out because they're afraid you'll take all the shine. Ok I'm done!).

What have the modern day plebs taught us? -That you can't really do anything applaudable with education if you lack wisdom and the lasting potential of cinder wood within your bowels. Wisdom burns as that fire that lights education up in flames! If you observe the traits of education, similar to the people and their thinking, it atrophies over time without wisdom--"if you don't use it you lose it." All of the education in the world can't save you if you have no guts to use it. Look at the masses of students who are graduating from colleges and universities all over the nation who haven't the slightest notion of how government works--not to mention what the original purpose of government was! But, these graduates with leaves for brains are allowed to manage public and private organizations because they hold a piece of paper that says they have some sense.

The only precursor to a true education: a student armed with a freewill and an opinion! Grade school is similar to what I imagine water boarding must feel like. As a child, every time I opened my mouth to speak they ushered me back into the principal's office. For twelve years, the energy within me set the light of the stars to shame, shining so bright sometimes that it blinded the objectivity of teachers and principles alike. I made a promise to myself that I would not bombard my students with that abuse, sparing them from a blindsided education. If they were ready for it, I would show them a way and if possible -- a way out.

The real test of education --and wisdom-- happens when students introduce their own expressive opinion without popular approval, especially the teacher's approval (anything else occurring in a classroom sounds like child's play to me). Mainstream opinions are okay for common people--but students worthy of their pay can't help but give a sigh of disapproval at every assertion of common people. For instance, they teach you in grade school and college, "cite, cite, cite"--not for the sake of giving credit where credit is due -- but, mainly as a way to show that you can garner the popular approval. The nod of your peers becomes a sort of Scooby snack. "Yes, yes, yes...my peers agree with me, I've been approved! This tradition of writing like that of opening the doors for women not only dates itself, but is classist, and feels like a pansy ass attack on individualism (People who support this type of mass production remind me of men who fight by swinging their arms in a windmill motion; Whenever I read nonfiction that list page after page of citations I think, did this person have an original thought to begin with?). How can I praise someone in my writing when there is none other like me? Yet, I flatter some till this day by conforming to this convention, if only not to experience what it feels like to have no voice in the world—an act of artistic expression! From experience, I've observed that it's the working class who finds it necessary to roll in cliques; they do everything in groups. So fucking social, they always need the regard of the group and people like this strike me as severely wrong. These basic types always roll in packs, don't they? The first sin of the working people is that they don't trust themselves. The 1 per centers, now there goes men and women who, if you hate for their wealth and snotty attitudes, you can at least give credit for trusting in their own diluted and psychologically sick view of the world. But with their dissolved sense of reality they code a world for themselves. If only the basic people of the world could code their own world with their own instructions and keep the rest of us who chose to abstain out of it! (Digression: Oh, but they have created this world haven't they? -They call it: the community. Oh the community.... If only I could finally rid my life of the community.)

But, what we find at the end of the tunnel is that education unto itself is pretty damn weak and useless and quite frankly, a scam on a worldwide basis. The only subject matters that hold any legitimacy today are science and math mainly due to the absence of subjectiveness (i.e. morality=fairy tales)--and even this latter assertion about math and science is not without question.

At the New York City Teaching Fellow's, their philosophy believes that education cannot effectively begin until "behavior is put in check." What do they concern themselves with education for? -Well, you can't create an obedient workforce with a bunch of disobedient potential can you? The billionaire Mayor knew this, his Leadership Academy (and their CEO principle) knew this; the Teaching Fellows knew this. With that said, someone might argue that a public school education might serve as more suitable for prisoners at Riker's Island and San Quentin than the youth of tomorrow. Either way, their tomorrow ties itself up with the "justice" system: "Being the education mayor, according to Bloomberg, has everything to do with management. Thus, he chose Joel Klein, a former Justice Department antitrust lawyer and non-educator he hired in July 2002. 'It's not an education job,' Bloomberg {said} bluntly. "(htt)

Even the university behaves as instructed today; it's become a factory for employee manufacturing. Before the modern day, only the wealthy enjoyed an education and utilized it in its original purpose--knowledge and wisdom, usually for the benefit of learning how to bring peoples to their knees, something to separate them from the rabble. Now, robbed of anything that made it interesting, the University cranks out "intellectuals" like McDonald's Happy Meals. When the working classes became eligible to flood the universities, universities prefabricated students for the sake of mass-producing a line of "educated" people ready for the labor market. Their presence didn't add any value to academia; it only spurred on that evil and mischievous notion of equality. Have I digressed here? -Not at all. Equality is a concept that is allowed to flourish in the universities--the manufacturing plants--in order to keep the people hopeful and satisfied. Even if the people never achieve a true sense of equality, what satisfies them most is the possibility of attaining it. The people never will attain equality for they don't have the guts to do what it takes to attain it. However, the fact that the upper classes allow them the ability to speak openly and confidently about equality satisfies them and robes them with a sense of power that they really don't have. It's no different than the slave masters or mistresses who forbid their slaves to read and write, but taught their slaves to read the bible. The sense of hope keeps the slaves happy and in the same manner puts out the flame of resistance. Why run away when you're treated so well? However, the reality is not so hopeful. For when these same students enter the work force, the realities are shocking and deforming. The workplace is not one of equality, but inequality. And if you go into it thinking otherwise, you'll find yourself on the bottom of the promotion ladder--if not fired.

What I witnessed in the Fellows program struck me as a mass class remaking of not only the students, but the teachers also: programs like the Fellows do not shy away from admitting that their primary diagnosis for the urban problem is treatment in the form of behavior modification. And that modification comes from "upper class" interest in order that the "lower classes" learn how to behave in their presence. Our jobs entailed breaking the student of his or hers natural inclinations and it began with breaking our own recalcitrant habits. This was our civic duty.

The next day I made sure I arrived at classes and trainings fifteen minutes early so as not to provoke any reaction from the program staff. I dressed the part: I arrived in a suit and tie. I put on the "white woman smile" when I passed by other Fellows and Fellow's staff. I did what it took to get a paycheck. I "played the game." Some other Fellows didn't fare so well. Later in the summer the classroom sulked more and more. Melancholy rested in the air. The heat outside sent us running into the classroom where the air conditioning worked improperly causing some of us to drop the act and resume our true personalities, as the heat will do sometimes. One night our coach sent the following email:

========================
6/25/13

From: Melissa Mancuso
To: Cedric Hines

I'm including this reminder about business casual dress, which connects to our norm to Be Professional. One way that we show how seriously we take our teaching careers is by dressing for success -think of it like formal register for your clothes. If you have any further questions about dress code, please see me or email me.

1. T-Shirts: T-Shirts are casual. We are a no t-shirt school – this includes fancy t-shirts with embellishments, or anything that looks like a t-shirt.

2. Skirt Length: Skirts and dresses should be no more than three fingers above the knee.

3. Pants: Must be dress pant material---no jeans/denim material, leggings, or anything too tight. Black Pants: If your black pants could look like stretchy pants or leggings from afar, don't wear them.

{5}. Maxi Dresses/ Flow-y Skirts: If it's casual enough to wear to a brunch on a weekend, it is not professional enough.

6. Sandals: No flip flops but ladies can wear business casual sandals– they usually have a back strap.

========================

For me, this email was a no brainer. Ever since I started working as a young man, my demeanor and presence always put white folks on edge. So, as to decrease their fear—and once again, as always, put their sense of the world before mine—I dressed the part. When white people feel that you look like them they let down their guard, but then the outright disrespect begins! (When they stop fearing you they step on you, whereas before they feared you, so they went behind your back to solve any workplace problems—so essentially, you were always fucked to begin with.) I went above and beyond and wore a full suit to work every day. I thought this should shut them up for sure, probably, maybe?

After the Teach Like a Champion viewing, the coach reiterated the email to us all. Some Fellows failed to follow the dress code that day, not because of disobedience, but because of financial constraints. One young lady whispered to me that a Fellows associate "threatened to drop her" from the program for her "choice of dress." It surprised me that she felt so comfortable divulging this information to me considering the environment engulfed us all in competition and fear. It was this fear that kept us from joining together to protest the humiliating email that degraded some fellows for being poor. Her eyes searched out mine as if she wanted to confirm whether I was one of "them" or had I still maintained my sense of self. "Can you believe that," she said, and I shrugged my shoulders. Unknowingly, we all have learned that when we enter an employment agreement that the agreement topples in favor of the employer. If they choose to fire you, they can always find another employee—but, if you quit, you can't always find another job. Yet, our society deems this fair. The employer owns you as property once you agree to work. Like cattle, which are stamped with a hot tool, you now belong to that organization.

I had already arrived at a dismal conclusion about this program, but I didn't want to nor did I think it wise to share this information. The Fellows program supplied a $2500 stipend for the summer. However after paying moving cost, rent in New York City, utilities and feeding oneself, the possibility of buying new work clothes seemed a luxury one couldn't afford.

A hand shot up in the air. The coach called on the young lady and she politely asked whether at any time in the future we would watch videos and receive training specifically geared towards students with disabilities in District 75. Ha! The class, in unison turned their heads back to the coach awaiting the coaches' response. The realities of the Fellows program dawned on everyone and it shocked me that she actually had the gall to ask the question. She spoke cautiously, "It seems all these videos are geared towards kids in charter schools, elementary schools in particular, but our kids are public school kids and many of us will teach middle and high school." She looked like she expected the worse from her question. It was a reasonable reaction; many questions were frowned upon and downright forbidden at the fellows. And for those who still had the nerve to ask these questions, their position in the program stood on shaky ground. However, she was right. All the schools shown thus far in the Teach Like a Champion videos showed kids dressed in uniforms at charter schools. The reason the Fellows placed us at Pace University and not uptown at Hunter college with other special education teachers, was to give us special instruction in teaching students in District 75--the most severely disabled students in the city (excepting those in a hospital setting). In fact, the books and instruction we received were exactly the same as those given to Hunter College teachers. So why was the Teaching Fellows providing a "special program" that was anything but specialized? The coach shook by the question stumbled on her words trying to remain dignified in front of the fellows for the sake of the programs reputation while at the same time maintaining honesty with her group of fellows. She performed well as a coach. She stood behind her podium looking out the door, up at the ceiling, down at her shoes, thinking of a politically correct answer. After a long silence, she finally agreed to bring in videos of her own related to our student population. This minor act of rebellion— her reluctance to lie for the Fellows—gained her our respect.

But, then a rupture occurred: the students weren't the only ones being prepared for an obedient future, so were the teachers! Now, we all realized what we were up against and the knowledge of it placed our morals in a duel against ourselves--get paid and shut up, or speak up and get fired.

CHAPTER 5: Post-R_____ America

In the summer of 2013 a different, but directly related type of duel took place. The verdict in the Trayvon Martin murder trial harrowed the nation in racial misunderstandings once again. George Zimmerman, a 28 year old mix-raced Hispanic man, who served as neighborhood watch for a gated community in Sanford, Florida, fatally shot 17 year old Trayvon Martin, a black high school teenager. July 13th marked a somber day for not only the Martin family, but more expensively (and expansively) for race relations in America. It served as another reminder among a multitude of past reinforcements of racism in America--the land of the freedom and equality. Despite these tenets of democracy, having black skin disagreed with America's idea of safety (black men still bring to mind images of America's dark past and the ghost that haunt this country). And the American government, a political body created so that men might think twice before harming another individual, continues to this day to permit and some might argue—condones—racial hatred and violence against young black boys and men. The trial and verdict hung over the country like an impending storm, and a chill went down the spine of our statehood; some wondered just how long? -- How much longer?

Bigots immediately reached for the "thug" card even though no evidence existed linking Trayvon to any illegal activity--and besides, isn't this what hypocrites do best? They sought to dehumanize Trayvon (and symbolically black men) by associating him with immoral acts. The first tactic bigots use is to link all black men with illegal activity, thereby insinuating that black men are by nature criminals—and therefore worthy of "justice". But what they've really done is demoralize black men. When you demoralize a man, you pressure him into a corner where he feels all hope is lost. In return, he fights for his life in ways that moral (self righteous) people don't have to. Instead, they stand in judgment. Here, we have the birth of a natural born criminal. But, the media couldn't do that to Trayvon because his life ended in the hands of a cold-blooded killer with absolutely no reason or authority for committing murder. Yet, the media still allowed negative imagery of Martin to fester throughout their objective storytelling to satisfy some need, any need no matter how irrational, to vilify black boys. This is America's post-racial society; this is the so-called progress we have struck open. This is "things getting better."

But let's remember that our post-slavery society (1890-1954) once stood for the separate but equal doctrine--which, justified and permitted separate treatment on the claim of equality--a doctrine that over time would supposedly improve race relations. It took sixty-four years after the infamous Brown v Board of Education Supreme Court ruling, for the United States to acknowledge that the policy only served to widen the racial divide. The socio-economic and, in this case, political divide between blacks and whites can't wait another sixty-four years. The little progress made in race relations so far has begun to take a 180 degree turn in the course of the events: Trayvon Martin and Michael Brown, to mention only two events out of a daily reality for black boys in America. The reluctance to face the ugliness of racism gives birth to a desperate situation in our country. While whites take back control of what they conceive as theirs--black bodies—their "white rage" displaces more and more black families -- with bullets. Even though statistics show that black males commit violent against other black males more so than the rest of society, we still perpetuate old ancient myths of a racial underclass.

White people want to maintain their sense of whiteness while our country continues to divide itself along the color line; the divide between white and black makes them feel different--and different equals good in their book--and I concur! Brown V. Board of Education struck a blow to that sense of identity. White people, men in particular, feel the need to take back what they, in their delusional historical imaginations, lost. They construct and contrast a glorious past with a terrifying future so long as the people of color exist freely side by side with them. In one instance, the white man both loves and hates the black man simultaneously. If only he could eat and gorge on his flesh and somehow digest him, maybe then, he could free himself of the love, lust, rage, and jealousy he holds within himself. He fails to conclude whether he prefers to imitate his nemesis or to kill him.

Let's analyze equality not as enabling but as a restrictive force. It's a dirty and malicious concept--on par with the belief in heaven and hell. Equality orders the breaks on our federal legislation. Just look at how our lame ass Congress intentionally stalled the mechanics of our government, from 2008-to the present year of 2014 and on, to get back at the first Black-American President whom they both hate (and secretly admire) for his proletarian policies -- policies aimed at leveling the playing field in this country for all peoples. The fight for equality deprives us all of peace and places us in a never-ending, and futile battle for what? -Some theoretical construct never achieved and which contradicts human history. Based on repeated attempts to resolve this issue in my mind I concluded that when you release yourself from the demands of equality and work in favor of a complete and resolute inequality, freedom takes on a clean and levitating feeling. Freedom washes itself from the sin of equality. The "state of nature" is brutal for those who, out of a lust for equality, fairness, and religious fervor, fail to prepare for it: those who suck on the tit of neoliberal nourishment -- equality, fairness, and "my brother's keeper" types. Where's a bib when you need it? The man of equality emulates the chains he places himself in. If only we could overcome this need for equality, we would surely find the key to our burden. And I, for the longest time fell to my knees often for this sin.

Look at our current President. The election of Barack Obama supposedly heralded the "post-r_____ America." Who presides over the post-racial America? Where is it? What does it look and smell like? I see the same old bullshit my grandfather saw, and his grandfather saw. Ask Andrew Young, the American politician, diplomat and civil rights legend, about the tea party movement and he'll all but tell you it's one sign the country hasn't reached a post-racial era. "Without making a moral judgment about it, let's just say ethnocentrism runs so deep in America that we are hardly beyond this," he said in an interview with ABCNews.com...The tea party "is motivated by a nativism -- an appeal to the good old days and people who are anxious about change and want to go back to the way they would like to think things were." (htt2) A Black President supposedly signified the environment had changed; that the incoming President granted blacks immunity from unabated, unjust attack and brutality by a bloodthirsty race. How can there be a post-r_____ America when the white race still salivates with a pathological focus on violence and destruction? (Has anyone on earth written about or read about a race so hell bent on destroying others than the American caucasian? Sometimes I just stand and observe the bestial behaviors of white American's and wonder why they love to see bloodshed.) I can't help but think it's apart of their firstborn instincts but I know very well it isn't; it's something that they've learned over time and just can't escape--a wrongful education. White America has no natural claim over violence but they act as if they do.

The only reason I get along with white people so well today is that I'm fully aware that I'm superior! -And get this, they hold the same feeling about me. No man seeks to compete against someone he thinks is equal to or below him. It's those above whom mankind always seeks to strive against. White rage is no exception. My superiority is surely not because of some fictional development in race relations that begins with an "e" (human nature doesn't change that fast). To add, racial superiority barricades and burrows itself in our nations capital so deeply that it would take three more civilizations on top of ours to rid us of the effects of its sickness. And so I become ever more sickly and deadly as I grow older and I spread my sickness without apology. Equality has been proven on numerous occasions to incite malevolence. Benevolence towards our fellow man organically comes about due to the further up and out our self-confidence soars. It's by promoting our inner experiences that we employ our greatest value in this life. This is what gains us the benevolence of the human race--not a race to show that we are created equal--because we are not!

July 14th, I attended my University class "Instructional Methods: Learning to Teach." The professor was an asshole like most: An upper thirty-ish white male who explicitly stated from the very beginning that the class would not go easy for anyone who didn't follow each and every instruction to the letter of the law. But, his lack of emotion and political correctness didn't bother me; his ignorance on the other hand couldn't escape my ridicule.

University professors walk the beat. They kill by lecture--literally and figuratively. Anyone whose ever sat through a college course knows the terror I speak of (such as drooling on your palm as you use it to hold up your weary head). In college today students don't learn how to use their own knowledge from within to enliven that which they learn in class; they learn how to use the knowledge meted out to them in rations for nothing—it's just a regurgitated mess. No need to say that the professor polices his student's voices. They learn when to raise their hand and when not, when to question the professor and how to question the professor. The modern day University pervasively and covertly instills in students behavior modifications necessary to operate in the work world, nothing else. Education today falls under the following definition: the mass production of the working class and how they must behave. The weapon of choice bears the only exception between the professor and law enforcement, the former inflicts an extensive mind fuck; at least the latter puts you out of your misery quickly. When the professor stands in his academic pulpit and professes his devotion to his craft, we don't believe him! -As soon as class is over, he's out the door before his own students. You hear in his tired jokes the remnants of an educator who once loved his job, but who arrives at the sad realization that his students often know just as much as he does —in particular, I speak of the liberal arts--for example, this professor, Peter Schmidt. Schmidt enrolled in the same Graduate Degree program that I excelled at four years prior before I decided to go for my second Masters. I could have stood behind that podium myself if I lacked a personality. I see no reason to hold my tongue--to look up to any man or woman as a role model--I never have, I never will. This includes the university Professor. He puts the charlatan to shame and he typifies the biggest charlatan in the education system. Jesus! I purchased my best education for free from public libraries. There, I gladly stumbled on great works of literature: e.g. Sexus, Plexus, and Nexus by Henry Miller. These tales stand as true inspiration and true instruction in the affairs of life.

One afternoon in July Professor Schmidt leaned against the podium with his back to the whiteboard with his sun burnt beard, baldhead, dressed in a casual flannel shirt and blue jeans. He opened his proud mouth and lectured from our textbook, Understanding By Design (UBD). UBD works as a backwards approach to lesson planning. The teacher begins by planning at the end, the big idea of the unit. Then going backwards he develops each individual lesson. According to the textbook, a teacher should use six facets to build assessment for understanding: 1. Explain 2. Interpret 3. Apply 4. Perspective 5. Empathy 6. Self-Knowledge. By the end of a unit a student should experience most, if not all, of these facets to truly obtain understanding of the subject matter. This text served as our guide for the rest of the summer.

Based on the rules he set at the beginning, and after having set the authoritative climate of the class, Schmidt made himself comfortable in his position of power--a little too comfortable for my taste. This day he allowed his true feelings to peak through, and his emotions laughed in the face of our political correctness.

To lesson the blow that his lecture would inflict, Schmidt started off explaining the six facets of understanding using an example from the Jewish holocaust. I sat in the back of the class with my back to wall reading the reports on my I-Phone about the Trayvon Martin verdict. During the break, I heard classmates talking about it. A good part of me already knew what the verdict would be based on our national pattern of devaluing the lives of black males but I read anyway. I didn't realize how much it would affect me. It hit me hard. I felt as if Trayvon jumped into my body at the moment I heard the verdict. I could feel his moans and his hurt, and I could have sworn I heard him weeping. He was I, and I was he, and he insufflated me with his spirit.

When Schmidt got to number 5, empathy, I looked up to look interested in his lecture. He shrugged his shoulders and said, "... Not all people involved in the Holocaust were evil". I thought, WTF (What the fuck?) You're telling me, the German citizens who watched as their Jewish, gay, and disabled neighbors headed towards the concentration camps weren't evil? Sure sounds evil to me! My internal antenna shot up at this point of the conversation detecting a one-two punch. And my conscience proved correct. I thought to myself he better not go where I think he's going. Like a Mack truck bearing down on I-95, he continued, "...Not all people involved in the slave trade were evil." As I turned my head left and right listening to his obscene, reckless, and totally oblivious analogy, I looked around in hope that somebody else might raise an objection before me, not leaving me alone in the line of fire as usual in circumstances like this--and as expected, no rebuttal from the class.

Having to speak for other people spins my anger out of control--I just want to speak for myself. But, often my voice inscribes itself on the minds of people whose backs languish against the ropes. They constitute a lazy bunch. This country is flooded with these free riders; they come to hate you for the same thing they loved you for, the ungrateful wretches. From experience, I've found that they don't have the nerve to speak up, but when those with strength stand up in the face of ignorance, the free riders feel as if they have the right to speak. "Oh he went too far; he could have spoke his peace in another way." These types cause bile to run out of my mouth. Nevertheless, someone must always speak up, even if only for their own sake. I stick cold and hard to the words of Anais Nan when she wrote," When you make a world tolerable for yourself, you make a world tolerable for others." And at the seed of that statement, my selfishness bloomed.

For, I know for a fact the underlying truth of this statement. I attended another class that summer where I had to call out the professor for one of those minor acts that many might say is an overexaggeration. No matter how often I raised my hand he looked over me. This blatant disregard for my opinion didn't sit well with me. Although I sat in the front row right next to the podium—the one he and other professors loved to lean on as if it nourished their demented cognition. No! No matter how many times I raised my hand he deliberately looked around, past, and through me; I was invisible--only until, like a phantom in the night did I, like a spook, rise up and call my own professors biases into question. I mention this anecdote not as a call for all students in higher education to quarrel with their professors, but only as an example of the voice within the voice needed to be seen and heard as a minority in academia. These little games that whites play in our post-r_____ America can and should not be overlooked--they should be called out each and every day they arise till the bastards get the point that you will not be a ghost forever. As a youth, my family and teachers talked about college like as if it guarded itself against bigots. Ha! The University houses some of the most educated bigots in the world. We often prepare our kids for a tough ride after college. I have an important news announcement for you all: The fight for respect of the minority begins when you enter the school system and grows stiffer and stiffer in resistance the more you advance.

After digesting the words that dribbled out of Schmidt's mouth, my hand shot up erect in the air like a Nazi, but I had no intention of pledging allegiance to his nonsense. "Did you just say that people involved in American slavery were not evil?" How in the hell could he justify this asinine statement? My voice shook, and my eyes strained to look him in the eye to see if he wholeheartedly believed what he said. "You're telling me that I should have empathy for the people who brought my people to this country, shackled, beaten, broken, and dehumanized?" After all we have been through in this nation, including the ending of slavery, Jim Crowe, lynching, and the civil rights movement, we still have peckerwoods like Schmidt around? I thought his kind rode off into the recesses of dark places like, Arizona. I said, "I don't care who you are, professor or not, that is just wrong and if you think I'm going to teach my students to empathize with a bunch of slave masters than you're out of your mind!" Grasping each side of my desk to balance my weight that became unsteadied due to the sting of racism--which, still shocks the nerves each time it's encountered-- and the fact that a professor of all people asked me to do the unthinkable. I lifted myself with the little strength I had up and out of his insidious lecture. As I walked out I saw the class looking back and forth from the professor to me as I made my way out the door.

In the hallway, I thought about a lot of things. Some related to what just occurred and some irrelevant. Every room in the hallway was closed and every Fellow trapped in their classrooms taking in instruction. It seemed to me through past and present experience that the man who sticks up for "the people" waste his time and energy--for the minds of the people houses mush to say the least. And after repeated threats to their livelihoods they hide their heads in the sand hoping for a better day. No such day is coming. Today's "civilization" is overwhelmed with branding themselves so as not to jeopardize their source of income. And it's not so far fetched to understand why. The employer and the employers lackey--the education system--can either make or break you if you allow them (and if you believe they can). For example, look at Atlanta Hawks co-owner Bruce Levenson. He admitted, that in 2012 he sent an email "implying that white fans are more valuable to him than black ones. 'My theory is that the black crowd scared away the whites and there are simply not enough affluent black fans to build a significant season ticket base,'Levenson wrote in the 2012 email to team executives." Levenson went on to say, "If you're angry about what I wrote, you should be," his statement said, "I'm angry at myself, too. It was inflammatory nonsense. We all may have subtle biases and preconceptions when it comes to race, but my role as a leader is to challenge them, not to validate or accommodate those who might hold them." (htt3)

Levenson would have gained more respect from this corner if he held onto his beliefs. It was Levenson's failure to believe in himself, which caused him to succumb to the wishes of the consumer-- to what he thought others could do to him--going so far as to apologize for his true feelings. He should have taken a note from the Donald Sterling journal. After being recorded using racially derogatory terms, Sterling was pushed to sell his ownership of the Los Angeles Clippers. He refused to apologize, however, which is more respectable seeing as we all know he's an old fossilized bigot. Unfortunately, many times the minority folds over backwards to appease the majority. Thinking back to Schmidt, only an ignorant educator would think to censor himself for the sake of his students. It's like voluntarily placing an iron muzzle over your mouth. Who can take such a man seriously? It's like the man who conceals his true opinions to keep his job! Seeing this situation with more clarity, I think professors and teachers who are censored disseminate a strong message: despite what they think, students indirectly learn to acquiesce in the face of alternative opinions. If we scatter seeds of timidness, what else can we expect to grow from the soil of the public education system?

I had to forgive myself for my actions that day. Who and what I fought for I'm not sure anymore?- The people? What have the people ever done for the outliers except ostracize us at every chance they get? The people, no matter if speaking about races, genders, and classes—has failed to do its job: to push social progress forward. As I lingered in the hallway, Schmidt's blank reaction and the class's mute response hung over me like a light fixture. And, as a fluorescent light bulb, an illumination moderately began to overlook me. Its light spoke about suppression and how suppression of an unacceptable opinion stands as a vicious tactic of the "do-gooder" types, not my kind. Its only purpose: to attack those inherently resistant (strong). Therefore, they prop up their ideal: the good students or the worker bee (aka the weak). I shamed myself for picking up such bad habits. Schmidt shared a moment of honesty with the class and revealed his inner truth just like Levenson did when he wrote that questionable email; but neither should have a gag order put on them for expressing their opinion. Just like a reader should not put this book down if I refer to both of them as pasty crackers! See--it's all in good fun! An individual's refusal to comply with today's politically correct society should not come under attack, but applause. Racism's ability to flourish lies in its ability to go unacknowledged. Racism is the bastard son of America: For so long, racism pitted us against each other because of an endless list of contradiction in values. When we finally become men and women who release inconsistent beliefs then the problem of the twenty-first century will not point its finger at the problem of the color line. (If you dislike black or white people you wont have to pretend otherwise.) Unity cries out for cold-hearted, unfiltered, honesty. You know you're a worker bee when the thought of resistance seems futile! I have more respect for a Schmidt or a Levenson than any of my classmates who sat there in silence--which, included students of color. Too many times have I found myself out there on the battle lines by myself when I should have remained on the sidelines.

As I sat down on the steps in front of one of the auditorium, I saw some students escape from their classrooms and scatter like sheep as they hurried to either the water fountain or the bathroom. Is this what we call a democracy? -A litter of obedient and willing worker bees? While in Greece in early 2014, I witnessed a true democracy in movement: Students and adults throwing off the scourge of apathy, protesting and voicing their concerns in the streets at the most inopportune and random moments. The students seemed to have their own language of civil disobedience that would fly over the heads of the American student. Lining the streets in one of Athens most famous centers, Monastiraki Square, burning flames to light up the ancient skies overlooking the city. That's living! That's Democracy--Randomness and actualization and mobilization of the human spirit. Today's American is totally opposed to this outlook. The American looks around and seeks approval before they act to see if it's okay to protest. LOL! Don't bother. "You are the weakest link!"

One major struggle of mine: offsetting two opposing concepts--a love of free speech in favor of an undue respect for authority. Going deeper, American citizens who tolerate censorship have also possessed too much patience for the germ that causes it: deep-rooted American religious intolerance. By religious intolerance, I mean the intolerance that religious people hold within themselves! A Schmidt and a Levenson didn't learn their racial beliefs out of a vacuum. American Christianity and racism spawn twin abominations sliding out of the same vaginal canal. The values of the former dictate the values of the latter--not vice versa. They say:" When the supreme court ruled out prayer in public schools—the steady downhill slide into the godless, immoral, valueless abyss that passes as education today, began 'A rape of our nations religious heritage, our national morality" (EDWARDS). These words ring true in the thoughts of many Christians today who are unabashed by this dearth of rationality, they muse on. However, let's not forget that this "national morality" originated from a religion that condones slavery, racism, and every other kind of ism' you can think of. Is it any wonder we can't get past race? It's going to take an act of nature to incite a change. But, looking at the big picture America gets off on silencing the disenfranchised: minorities and the poor. Our society prides itself on its awareness of racism but fails at every turn to do anything about it: we transmute prejudice, institutional and structural racism, but it's still all talk! If our society truly wanted to change it would have risen to the occasion already—" this would require white people to look at themselves, something they have been stubborn to do." (Baldwin.) Educated and wealthy citizens feel it sets them apart and distinguishes them as the bird that drifts from the flock; unfortunately the days of the true aristocrat have long flown away! True aristocrats don't fly our skies anymore; the pseudo aristocrats today languish in the days of old when their skin color could buy them an edge. In the twenty-first century that check has been cashed and that account overdrawn.

I remember the way the class froze as I walked out. It wasn't the first time I've broken through ice barriers. Without turning around, I could see their eyes following each step I took out the door; apart of them wanted to come with me, but instead spurned me. They sat still as a frame on a wall opposed to my behavior-And who's to blame them? At some point, our indoctrination takes hold of us. Only few of us escape it and guess where we end up? -Either on the boards of fortune five companies or in maximum-security prisons. Providing for our families to feed, clothe, and house them, undergirds every action we take. Our need to provide for others governs our bred instincts. So, when my classmates sat there, taking in the lesson, taking notes, honoring the legendary code of denial-while I walked out of all of it--they simply rationalized their behavior as a form of survival; or better yet, they fell in line.

Do-gooders say free speech won't survive if one person's speech suppresses that of another. Eureka! -We're talking about individuals, not groups of people. The people as an entity not only skirt the table of the deserving, but stand completely outside the political process; it's only by temporary, violent, illegal, unethical, outburst do they take part in the political process; and, as the occasional riot aspirates its last empty battle cry the system returns to usual. We only seldom hear the voice of the people when they come together and use their power of numbers to force their will on society. Otherwise, like an inebriated family member at Christmas dinner, nobody pays them any attention.

And here, we delve a little deeper into the psychology of this class. Free speech at the core represents an insurrectionary act. It expresses a voice for those who lead, and as a result, represses speech for those who follow! -Anything else falls under the "offense principle": it's an offense for ordinary people to speak as the distinguished. You hear it all too often—"be all you can be": Low class propaganda! The way I see it, my class, If I may use them as representative of the people of the nation, took offense at the thought of speaking up and expressing their own opinion—an act beyond their capability--and their right. Caught in between two leaders they inwardly sided with me but outwardly sided with the professor. Remaining quiet provided safety and aren't they always looking for what's safe? We all know their type. Whenever someone they know chooses not to go the prescribed route—they label them as "crazy" or "lazy." But, the working class works their butts off to overcompensate the laziest bunch of people on the earth; they prescribe mediocre remedies for an epidemic. I have to say as a unit and a class they block the right to free speech. Turn your attention to those who inwardly supported the Occupy protest, but did little to outwardly support it for fear of retribution. I must have looked like some rabble-rouser to them! We know the fate of such people: rabble-rousers always succumb to suppression in the end. My free speech censored the opinions of another, the professor. We fomented agitators, we agitate each other--but don't true spirits always do this? I look forward to the day when the ideals of the freedom of expression will have found a true home in the mouth of their rightful owners: individuals. Only when those who have the right to speak, speak-up, will progress have found its final resting place. And so nobody can blame the class for remaining silent. For them, I leave this last advice: freedom of expression is a precursor to (**CENSORED CONTENT**)

When people have become accustomed to mistreatment so long they come to believe they deserve it. Just look at the way the Republican Party speaks about gays--openly and proudly. As a result you have many gays who feel compelled to remain in a defensive position, expecting harassment from such groups. However, this is a form of weakness--for a defensive position is the weakest position. However you have those who think their empowered by this position but all they gain is an insecurity complex that day in and day out sends the message: you have to defend yourself. NO! Be yourself! I say walk into the most conservative gathering places, kiss, fondle and do everything else under the sun with your lover that would constitute a crime in many southern states. Preempt the bigots! Catch them off guard. While riding the subway--pull out gay pornographic material with explicit acts on the cover. While at the bus stop speak ill of that heterosexual family, which thinks it's their right to make you stand while they sit--and do not by any means, move out of your seat to make due for the family! The individual is way more valuable and worthy than the spread of vermin: i.e. children. Why? -What does the American people do when the rights of minorities are violated: bury the issue with the victim. I wonder with hopelessness how long will this not-so secret hatred lie underground to await a proper burial? My colleague's reaction made me aware of what I had already known from past encounters with bigotry: one, like always I'm alone; and two, that justice abuses its sons who refuse to submit to belittlement. (For there is no justice.) Marginalization was my prize, and mine alone. I didn't overreach—I did my duty and mine alone--to speak-up, always, and into the undecided future.

The next day towards the end of class, Schmidt called me to the podium. Composed and ready to present his case, and on his terms—well after the incident--he asked, " Why did you storm out of class?" We stood there two grown men staring each other down, eye to eye. The class dispersed slower than usual as bystanders tried to grasp pieces of our conversation to see who would get the upper hand in the standoff. Putting on my backpack I searched for the right words. In times like these I learned that I needed to spy on myself searching out every word and phrase before it came out of my mouth knowing people in authority love to use your words against you. "I didn't agree with you," the words jolted out in an angry black man tone. I guess my anger hadn't subsided. I didn't like the feeling of this situation. I didn't like him. I didn't like the idea that he felt comfortable approaching me about a wrong he committed asking of me a rationalization for my actions. I stood there waiting for him to give me a rationalization for his asinine comments! I squinted my eyes and looked through him--as I had already been in situations like this before and knew very well the tactics used by those in power to make one question himself. I was willing to go down in a psychological entanglement.

This situation transported me back to my sophomore year at the University of California, Davis. A small college town outside the Sacramento area, Davis is known for two populations: its students and its cows. It's a city where young men and women consider tipping over defenseless cows, fun. Like any college town, the students drunk to excess to prove something to either themselves or one of the many fraternities and soro's around. For those who drive, it's a difficult city to navigate because almost everyone has a bike and you just want to hate them in all their confidence, especially the way they ride through the streets as if they had bumpers for butts. A town full of "liberals", everyone considers themselves open minded. I hate the term open-minded--for when I hear people describe themselves with this term it simply gives me a clue to how close-minded they were at some point, and how they must have some lingering closed-mindedness within them. Often liberals can be the most innate bigots.

Walking out of my Anthropology class one day, the professor, an older white male, somewhere in his sixties, approached me at the end of class. It surprised me as the classroom held more than two hundred students. And no matter how honored I acted that he knew my name it's still unusual for a professor to remember each student's name—especially a student whom the professor never met. He stepped cautiously towards me in the most composed manner. "Mr. Hines can I speak with you," he said. "Yes," I responded suspectfully. He sighed and looked at me. "Did you call one of my graduate students an uhh," he paused, " a mutherfucker?" I paused because I wanted to burst out laughing at his sterile and professional use of the word "mutherfucker." I retorted, "No, I said this is a bunch of muthafuckin bullshit!" He looked at me in that unapproving, paternalistic manner in which white authorities have looked at me since a very young age. "This is unacceptable," he said. And he hit a nerve. Once again, the education system had suspended me from their belief system and left me dangling. I think "Unacceptable" dons an ugly name, one of those words white people call us when they want to say" Nigger!" I continued, "Yea I said it." I didn't see the need to half step or moderate my words. He dug a lot out of me with the least amount of words. I wanted him to roll in those words like swine. The incident he referred to occurred not more than a week before. One of the graduate students, a Chinese national, graded me, in my view, unfairly on an essay. So, I approached him about it. We spoke about it and he refused to acknowledge my complaint or to reconsider the points I made in my essay. The professor gave me a long story about the graduate student's culture, how in China behavior like mine received severe punishment, and that I made the graduate student fear for his safety. This wasn't the first time I made someone "fear for his or her safety". My birth onto this earth alone caused many to fear for their safety: Black man! Black man! Run! This situation, all too familiar presented itself like a test of my resolve. The heavens were playing a joke on me seeing whether I had lost my resolve to stand up for myself. I knew this test; I constantly encountered it in middle school and high school. When a young black student challenges a teacher, or any authority for that matter, about the value of his work--and oftentimes his life-- teachers turn them down. Black students aren't supposed to complain. No, they expect us to take what they give us and shut up. Sorry, not this one! For so long I demanded my respect from the educational institutions and the prices I paid almost toppled me into academic bankruptcy. Too often my resolve was challenged and I usually came out on top—after having disciplined them muthafuckas! The University newspaper posted my case in the crime section of the news without displaying my name. "Student verbally assaults graduate student," it stated. From that day onward for more than two months the University forced me into the student affairs office where I would either apologize or they would expel me from the University. I refused for many weeks. I sat in the office one hour at a time in silence with the student affairs official. It wasn't until I got tired of coming to the Universities' version of a justice department that I finally apologized just to get the matter over with. It may seem a destructive path for many and an ineffective way to get things done; but when you have nothing to lose—and your horizons faded out before you got a chance to reach them—then only if your tough as steel do you cut a swath through these obstacles at any cost. No footprints charter your course. You're on your own. Survival for those of us who don't want to just "get by," starts here.

There, I stood in front of Schmidt squaring off once again with another white man standing in my way. "You know," he said, "I didn't mean to insinuate anything about race or racism." I laughed inside. I realized his attempt at backing off from the situation and I didn't want to pursue it any further seeing I had won so I assisted him and cooling off the tension. We played that politically correct game you must play at the University and the work place with white people and he played it back with me.

Before I turned to get the hell out of there, he gave me the gift of warning, "This situation will not go over very well if you do anything like this at the Department of Education, Cedric." I looked into his eyes knowing very well what he meant and that the verity of the statement would prove true and that I would once again spit in the face of belittlement.

CHAPTER 6: The-Job Hunt-P.S.226M

I succeeded in having a voice at Pace University to some degree,
but with no telling if this would work at the New York City
Department of Education (DOE). And my first interview with PS
226M didn't help to quell this indecision. I attended a District 75
job fair for teachers downtown in the Battery Park area of the
city. This part of Lower Manhattan, below Wall St., gives the
impression of a city within another city--very stand offish and set
to the side as if it owned itself; the West Side Highway cuts
through it separating it from the rest of the financial district.
Almost all of the District 75 Teaching Fellows who had not
secured jobs yet attended the fair. The fair took one whole floor
of the building. Classrooms served as interviewing locations
while Fellows lined up outside the classrooms to get their chance
to have a one-on-one interview with the school representatives.
Some schools sent staff members to interview; some principles
attended in person to represent their schools.

After interviewing with one potential school based in Harlem, I
decided to take a chance with PS 226M. I stood in line as one
after another teaching fellows walked out with a confused
expressions; I asked one of the fellows how she thought it went
and she commented that the principle looked "mean as hell" and
went on about how she didn't get a good vibe from her. Two
other fellows would walk out with similar, or worse, impressions.
I didn't let this discourage me. I've met many people who scowl
and in retrospect reflect some of the best people you'll ever
meet--so, with confidence I proceeded with my interview.

Inside, like an attack dog and its master, sat Shelly (Rachel)
Klainberg, Principle, and Jeanne Bradley, Assistant principle.
When I entered the classroom I immediately proceeded to give
them eye contact to gauge them. Shelly, a Jewish woman in her
late 40's (I aged her by one teacher who said her age floated
somewhere in the 30s, but as looks go...) sat at the corner of the
table composed with her hands on her lap dressed in grey slacks
and a black long sleeve shirt looking very conservative. Her short
haircut--which, gave an impression I doubt she intended to give
—whispered LESBIAN. I thought, hey cool, maybe we might
have something in common as nothing in her demeanor or
presentation hinted at any other commonality. Behind her at the
same side of the table heeled Jeanne; a plump white lady, her

face made her look like she was in her late 30's and her short haircut said, "I'm aging, but please card me." A bubbly woman, she smiled often and without reason. They played good cop, bad cop. The prospects didn't look good for me.

But, life is funny because if I think back on my past employers, some of the most repulsive bosses often employ a comforting mask. They often hide behind their assistants-or overseers--who tend to enact more vile punishments than the boss could ever conceive. With smiles as deplorable as their motives, they move about in a masquerade to keep you off guard. There's no such thing as a friendly boss. The moment you think they are one of the "good ones," you'll slip and run off at the mouth revealing information that can and will alienate you. All employees and bosses at some point become disaffecting or like pleasant adversaries.

At the end of the interview, Shelly's demeanor changed for the better; she smiled. Actually the two, both smiling, shook my hand and stated that they liked my responses and my resume and thought I might go forward as a good candidate. We set up another interview for me to do a practice run in front of the students.

After succeeding in the first interview, I knew life had a sense of humor. I thought the worst about Shelly when I walked in and look what happened. In my mid twenties I worked for a severely depressed man who built a non-profit organization from the ground up. In the mornings you knew when he walked in: all side conversations halted. It pleased him to see his staff stoop down to share his misery--but the rules of the game seized us all to the point that our first instinct's evaded his detection—meaning, we stayed out of the way of his wrath. We understood our position. It's bosses who release their workforce from the imprisonment of positive expectation (expecting decency)-- it's these that represent the most agreeable bosses. I mean bosses who acquiesce to insanity and who don't mask their madness. They "wupp" us into shape. The thought of a "good boss" makes me chuckle. I've found my best employers at heart unpleasant. The discomfort their arbitrary reasoning portends is a disagreeable feeling because the employee never knows what they want. You never know what the expectation is; every attempt at satisfying the requirements of the job earns you a verbal or written lashing.

You can't win. It's fun for them. I prefer the management, which can fire at will for no reason at all. At the least you die only one death. In addition, you're thankful for even the harshest punishment for it at least signals what you shouldn't do next time.

It's the entitled government jobs that violate the laws of labor. Still somewhat of a new phenomenon, this desire for "good" bosses reeks of a slave mentality dressed up in a neo-liberal costume. In the past, bosses freely exercised racist, misogynistic, homophobic and all viewpoints bigoted without retribution. Now, the laws have turned their back on management so now they must disguise their ignorance and bigotry. I blame neo-liberals: they've helped to mask the macabre conditions of working labor. The reality can't mask the inner contradictions: that workers want and prey to like their jobs especially when they receive pay raises and promotions! Wow, a two percent raise, they say. Now, I can afford to actually pay my rent—and—maybe catch a movie? Working gives them a sense of purpose and I don't think anyone should deprive them of this need; nevertheless, in direct contradiction, they can't seem to escape that bruise of conscious which whispers in a prophetic manner that they will never overcome the 9-5. And they soon believe it. Even if they do overcome the workplace, what will they do with themselves? People with a "good work ethic" don't know how to enjoy leisure, only the extremely rich and the extremely poor know (e.g. dependence on wealth and welfare to go about doing what one really wants to do in life-- it's only the working class who feel the need to work, work, work in order to feel complete).

Yet, we hop from job to job seeking that tolerable boss whom we might like and learn to enjoy and the job that will finally make us feel like winners. I can't count how many conversations I've engaged in with people who remain hopeful concerning the working man's predicament. "If only management would treat their employees right," they say, "then their employees would be more productive and actually enjoy their work." What kind of shit is this? It's like blatantly admitting that the workplace is a slave plantation--but only if management would make it bearable, we could place a beautiful sepulcher around it to make it look appealing. But, at some point their reality will set it-- whether it is at a young age or in old age--which, will say that the work place leads to death.

I stumbled on PS 226M on a hot August day and my skin boiled with sweat, but I knew bearing the heat outside would provide financial shade in the long run thinking of how well the first interview ended. However, when I arrived, the scene horrified me. It looked like the school once dawned an air of respect for an institution of education, but like a child let down from countless withdrawn promises, the school looked sad. I climb the hot steps to reach the third floor of the school site. The room where Shelly and another assistant principle, Imma Jardi sat was consumed by minimalism: just one round table with a desk behind it. I thought I was the desperate one who needed a job, but the appearance of the school cried out for help too. Their situation looked just as desperate as mine.

I entered the class boldly while Shelly and Imma remained in my shadow. Three students sat with two paraprofessionals (state required employees who assist with the students and teachers needs). Imma owned a serious demeanor just like Shelly. They came from behind me and haphazardly put together some desk and a portable white board for me to do my lesson. I practiced my lesson beforehand countless times so I knew what to do, yet, my attention swayed back and forth between the students and the inconceivable facial expressions on Imma and Shelly's faces.

Unsurprisingly, I excelled at the interview. Imma and Shelly took me back to the office and raved about how well I did. They offered me the job on the spot. Like a scripted play it went off without a problem. Imma leaned over, with both palms on the table, in a manner intended to show me her sincerity. She spoke with me like a child who just went out for Peewee tryouts like she wanted to instill in me her confidence. I played along with it as if I didn't overflow with confidence. But, I let her feel like she was giving me something I didn't already possess. She seemed to get wet at the notion of teaching adults. Like she didn't know much herself but as soon as she did learn a new tidbit of knowledge, she waved it in everyone's faces. But, I didn't need her paltry self-help crumbs.

The other Fellows were different. I remember many of them parading their new employment in front of other Fellows who had not yet found a job. In their celebration I saw that seizing a new job amounted to all the gratification they needed. It made them feel complete and accepted. I feel sorry for employees who don't possess themselves. The power employers exert over employees can amount to emotional abuse. No, this isn't hyperbole! I could definitely tell that both administrators knew to set a tone that reflected their everyday work habits, an emotional push and pull that swept up anybody who dared resist. However, for the moment the decision pleased me. So, I accepted the job. I was a New York City Teacher.

The first day of school for teachers landed on September 3rd, I arrived at the school eager to get started. We held our first faculty meeting in the hallway. The whole arrangement of the meeting hinted at a haphazard scramble; I never attended a meeting in a hallway with chairs and no desk. On top of that I inquired of Shelly a week before classes started, when she would provide the curriculums. She emailed back that the school provided curriculum maps on the 3rd; however, the administration didn't provide them until October. So, what the fuck should I have taught for an entire month? A whole month passed by while the class and I completed worksheets-which, I printed out of a coloring book to look busy. I didn't know what my students could do, so I was told that I should "assess my students," but never given any training on how. Did it matter to them much that the classes learned little if anything?

I couldn't complain much; my employment provided for me a new apartment, new clothes, and a new lifestyle in New York. And that made me feel somewhat safe. At the same time I found myself constantly trying to read the emotions of Shelly that day and how the year would play out; it left me in a tenuous position. It's funny how we take jobs to feel comfortable and safe (i.e., safe from homelessness) and after the initial excitement ceases we are launched into a never ending cycle of fear and suffering--mainly from the thoughts of losing what we gained. We assume that settling down into a steady job exhibits good qualities of maturity. Yet, the moment we settle, our world loosens at the seams and leaves us in a tenuous circumstance--forever at risk.

CHAPTER 7: The Masks Fall Off

Fear occupies an inordinate amount of our time, but that does not make it our salvation! We wake up everyday with it on our minds in some form or way wondering if we will prove good enough to move to the next level on the job--or if we will maintain our jobs or be let go. Fear pushes us further and further, right and left--anywhere--but somewhere. Knowing very well deep down inside that all fears tells tall tales. As humans beaten down by the labor market we still believe in it since we haven't known anything else since birth--wake up, go to the job, get off, relax and consume television (another part of the production process), then, back to the job. Straying from this pattern leads to suffering—and attacks from those too afraid to deviate from this path—for fear feeds and nourishes selflessness and hopelessness. How many people will read this book and consider ever raising their voice in the workplace? As a result, fearlessness has closed its door on many of us--our initiation, rescinded, until we learn how to wear our lives inappropriately.

Put it like this: the condition, which separates humans from a sea stack is that these rocks contain enough intelligence to sit still. Rocks are smart enough to know that fear and moving about like a rolling stone won't preserve it from the thrashing waves of the sea. No amount of resistance could relieve us of the conditions we create for ourselves the moment we kneel in the workplace. We hang hope on the cross everyday because of our dependence on living and working-- as if the job could save us. For, how long shall we wait? How long? Often we think our jobs set us aside or up on some pedestal--some people take up positions of "honor" such as that of teachers, lawyers, social workers and the like to eventually end their careers with the feeling of having made a difference, LOL! Surprise. The same problems you wasted your life away tackling will outlive you! When you leave this earth those same problems you fought to solve will provide the future generations with something to keep them busy! --While they await death.

A month into this job a revelation appeared to me: staff members juggle this fear too. The teachers and staff bore an unbelievable and extreme fear whenever an administrator suddenly appeared. For instance, when the day came for all teachers to have their bulletin boards plastered with students work samples, a couple of the teachers rushed to me with speed and trepidation not for themselves, but for me. They said my wall, "Didn't look up to par," and as a result Shelly would come down on me like a lightening bolt. I thought they overreacted. They all shared stories of her anger the previous year and how she cursed some staff out. This I couldn't imagine. Her asceticism made her appear somewhat Stoic. She didn't let one hair on her head move without critiquing and thinking about other ways she could have prevented her hair from falling out of place, she would probably ask herself, "What are the next steps my hair follicles will take?" I didn't know what to believe, but at so early a point in my career I didn't want to disappoint so I changed the wall over three times. I still couldn't gather my thoughts together to think that the well-composed lady I met in two interviews would suddenly morph into a raving mad woman. And the naive part of me believed she understood that the Assistant principles failed to pass down any real curriculums —in actuality, no teacher received a curriculum for the first month. The truth says that we all die everyday on the job. Why not die fighting? —That's what I call a lesson! When I looked at my coworkers I saw a mob of potential warriors backing away from every fight. The fear I witnessed eerily reminded me of my own destiny. If Shelly could play a part in my impending doom, than at least I should wear horns for the occasion. For in life countless other Shelly's will pop up like roaches. The time was now. Hiding in the shadows couldn't save me. The janitor, who earned over 80k for pushing and shoving a mop around at the end of the day, lived with more life than the teachers at that school. He should have taught us! I can't help but imagine that he made it by dealing with nothing but bullshit.

Every month, all of the staff attended a staff development day that focused on instilling the tenets of the Danielson Rubric--a new evaluation tool used (abused) to ascertain the functioning level of a teacher. But, I learned something much more interesting about PS 226M at the next meeting. In our November staff development meeting Jeanne led. If you've ever seen a wind up toy, Jeanne's probably a distant relative: Scripted like a Tyler Perry screenplay, she's predictable and tiresome. Just watching her, which requires more than two eyes, makes you spontaneously lift your hands and say, "I give up." She tried so hard to earn cool points even going to the extant of joking about using cocaine in her spare time. (From what I heard, that wasn't the first time she joked in front of other teachers and staff about such extra-curricular activities—but that's all heresy LOL.). This was one of her faces.

As she readied the crowd for her lecture, we sank down in our seats preparing ourselves for the worse. Her voice and body twisted each and every way trying to appease us, but we didn't want to hear anything she had to say, knowing very well she was a beast--and a two-faced beast at that. She was known for laughing and joking with teachers and then days later calling those same teachers into Shelly's office for "inappropriate behavior. " To add, this mongrel couldn't explain one of our questions about the evaluation rubric without referring to the words on the screen. We could read already! We needed an explanation for an evaluation, which nobody, including the teachers and administrators, nor the Union, knew anything about. Yet, our jobs depended on it. She moved about the front of the classroom constantly pointing back to the overhead as if we were dogs looking at our own shit and as if she employed a new teaching technique she just learned from an online teaching course. As she saw the crowd become restless I saw her plastic smile fall back into an organic, hateful position. Although angry, she still managed to outwardly keep it in check, but her eyes hollered something else. Then I saw her second face.

We returned from a quick break and another round started. As I sat back down into my seat I saw one of the younger teachers silently shedding tears. Jeanne admonished her about her work during the intervening break, but the teacher wouldn't go into any more detail than that. The meeting went on despite her tears, actually in front of her and only I and one other staff member asked her, "Are you okay?" Then, Jeanne lashed out. Her questions flew at any and every staff member hoping to trip them up. She saw that the sobbing teacher would not stop crying so she went in further out of embarrassment or carelessness. Jeanne stood right in front of her and she continued to berate the teacher with questions. Each question encouraged more and more tears to the point that even I got angry. "Huh, huh, huh?" she asked again and again waiting for a reply standing with her left hand on her hip. She shot two quick and hard questions at me, but I took them and laid her assault to sleep. After what seemed an exhausting period of time, she seemed tired of trying to outwit us so she sat down and looked at us recomposing herself as she had become emotionally untangled. I saw her third face.

The staff watched, but nobody said a word about it. They desensitized themselves to this type of treatment and knew the rules of the game very well. Acts of insensitivity such as this made survival for teachers at 226M a sad affair and would become routine for administrators--it acted as a means of control, and indeed, it worked! Showing strength sometimes reveals the sense of a lack of control within an institution. When you show all of your cards, you have nothing else to play and Jeanne often found herself in this position. If you use abuse as your first and last resort, what else can you do? Verbally abusing this teacher only uncovered her weak and pathetic disposition. Her kind always reaches for a ballistic missile when a slap on the wrist suffices. Big and bad--or just a big bitch--does not make one invincible.

Authority figures in decline like Jeanne hunt for insubordination everywhere. Everywhere terror strikes them--will the workers unite and create a strong resistance? They hunt through the entire school for employees who question their intentions. Nobody knows whom to trust because spies lurk everywhere like roaches. The whole system turns against itself perverting everyone involved: I wanted to say-- the kids, remember the kids? At 226M, here lies the equation of authority: order and abuse equal strength. However, this mistreatment inadvertently created a resistance. It swept us up in something greater than all of us combined. If belittling a grown woman at a staff "development" day meant strength, then Jeanne achieved her objectives above and beyond the call of duty. She symbolized an authoritative regime. More and more the truth surfaced: that the school leaders I interviewed with revealed themselves to actually be more conservative than anyone could have imagined. The lack of charisma and personality between Shelly, Imma, and Jeanne and their efforts to maintain the status quo solidified them in my imagination as the instillers of fear. Their types have been around for a long time. Their symbol of authority crept its way into our way of life a long time ago. It goes back to what Marxist considered a division of labor: In capitalist society, division of labor is biased towards social classes, and the upper classes use management techniques such as Taylorism, and bureaucracy, to essentially subdue the workers, leading to alienation, and poor working conditions." (htt4).

The reckless meeting came to an end and I gathered up my belongings in my classroom and prepared to head out, and I had the pleasure of running into Jeanne. She saw me talking to the teacher who had wept during the meeting and we exchanged uncomfortable glances until I realized that she didn't look at me the same anymore. She saw that I wore the same face day in and day out. Unfortunately for me, I made a mistake speaking with the other teacher so soon after the mayhem as associating with the weak tends to breed weakness in you. It's like an infectious disease and you can never expect help from those you help.

As Jeanne walked out, she said, "Have a good weekend, Cedric," with no smile. The show ended and her colorful masks fell off revealing something altogether opposed to the image I remembered from the job fair.

CHAPTER 8: Grading The Teacher

Soon, the fall left as soon as it had came, and with it my patience. "Where is the administration? I need help."--I yelled out loud to myself.

Luckily for me, the only senior teacher left among all the teachers drew me into her confidence. H----, a tenured teacher of advanced years disburdened me with her inappropriate sense of humor. She had this way of mimicking some of the disabled children that was so out of line, and at the same time hilarious. She would tilt her head to the side as she started mimicking someone having a seizure as she flailed her hands and arms in the air. She carried herself in an approachable manner and never fell short of laughter and jokes. An older Jewish lady, who lived on the Upper East Side not far from 226M, her words cut deep and her tongue filleted. She popped in and out of my class and often asked whether I needed help knowing very well I did. She dropped in with books and materials without having to ask her for them. Other teachers would help out the same. If not for the other teachers, Shelly might have discarded me sooner. It's a fact that teachers defend the teaching profession when nobody else will—standing in as the glue that holds the school in tact. It made me wonder what use the administration served. What did they accomplish besides perfecting the lash of the whip? They never paid any visits when you needed them; then, when they would surface out of a cloud of confusion they muddied the situation even more so. We often thought things couldn't get any worse, but our nightmares dreamed too small.

My classroom looked ill prepared for instruction: In the back, a lonely library of books inaccessible to many general education students, for some reason lined my library shelf. My students didn't read at a kindergarten level--they read at a pre-kindergarten level. One of them hadn't even learned that a book goes from left to right and the others were still learning that pictures and words in a book have meaning. Basic is an understatement. They couldn't prepare themselves for what this administration had in mind for them neither could I. What else did I have? I had a smart board that nobody in the Teaching Fellows or the school ever taught us fellows to use. So, essentially what I had was a fancy but useless screen--somewhat similar to the dreams Shelly and Imma sold me in the interview. My class lacked in all quarters: next to zero pens, pencils, and writing paper to help students access the basics and when I asked Jerry, the unit leader, for supplies, I met face to face with stiff resistance. He watched over that supply closet like the Abominable Snowman--he resembled the snowman too! Swinging his arms around his waistline he would walk in to my classroom complaining about any and everything. He knew half of what I knew about the school and he had been there for many of years. Without the schools help I paid out of pocket over $600 of my own cash on student supplies that first month. It helped little since I didn't have a clue of what to teach! I made due with what I had.

Every day I came to work I labored under frightening conditions. I didn't know what day the administrators would charge into my classroom to evaluate me. For informal evaluations, they could come at any time they wished--even while you were walking your students to the lunchroom--to evaluate your teaching practice. I didn't know what to teach so I went on the New York State common core website and other New York State websites to determine the scope of learning for students in the 8th and 9th grades. The curriculum maps--or curriculum as the school called it--consisted of inappropriate subjects gathered haphazardly by the assistant principle in charge of English, Jeanne Bradley. For instance, looking at the following unit: Reader's Workshop

Day 1: Readers are introduced to selecting books and enjoying silent reading
Day 5: Readers learn and listen to each other and share effectively with a partner
Day 11: Readers learn to orally recommend books to others by telling about the main idea/s of the book
Day 13: Readers identify and list different kinds of fiction

Let's evaluate these daily topics. Day 1: as stated before, not only could my students not read. Day 5: my students were non-verbal--which shows just how disconnected the administrators were from my classroom. Secondly, as Autistic students, sharing was a hindrance by virtue of their condition, which meant I had to somehow teach them how to overcome Autism at the same time I was teaching academics. Day 11: How could my students tell about the main idea of a book if they didn't know what the words of a book meant? Or, without me reading the book for them? -Or without someone else, like the teacher, telling them what the book was about--in which case, they are not readers, they are listeners. Day 13: HOW IN THE HELL CAN YOU DISCERN BETWEEN FICTION AND NON-FICTION IF YOU CAN'T READ? -OR, IF YOU HAVE A CONDITION THAT CREATES DIFFICULTIES IN DISCERNING BETWEEN ANIMATE AND INANIMATE OBJECTS? For some of my students, the stories of Harry Potter could very well be non-fiction. And so, I started to see why there was constant turnover in my classroom.

The rate at which teachers in past years left my class provided evidence that the only support administration gives at 226M favors pushing the revolving door for you when you leave. This system must have sustained itself for some time. A parent of mine made sure to state, on two different occasions via email, and in person, that his son had four different teachers in four years (see supporting documentation). Not to mention the staff informed me that the four years prior Shelly had hired a male teacher (apparently a token in a system dominated by brute women with an awkward view of feminism), then nudged the male teacher to leave at the end of the year—indirectly nudged of course. What causes teacher turnover? Providing the minimal level of educational support. Teachers leave for one reason: administrators have folded the patience of the teacher over and over onto itself to the point of non-existence! (P.S. you think you're going to treat teachers like the slime on the bottom of a New York City garbage truck and think teachers won't treat your students and children so? Not that I ever have or wished to, but waxing realistic, some teachers might think otherwise. Think about it, they're with your children seven hours of the day probably longer than they spend with their parents in a day.)

For schools that care, decreasing teacher turnover starts with helping teachers help themselves, thereby perpetuating health and happiness. The current system seems so eager to help teachers blast students out of their ignorance with a magic wand (e.g. by dictating how a teacher should structure every minute of their class instruction thereby successfully morphing the classroom into a production line for both the teacher and the student). Their view of teaching looks down on the teacher as some temporary expense that they tolerate for a time. As earlier in this story when I mentioned that my friend Latoya's employer

planned to replace employees with a computer program—
officials from city hall down to school administrations hold the
same view of the schools—wishing that a program might one day
replace teachers! For instance, the new Danielson Evaluation
Rubric discredits teachers who talk a lot. Principals use the
rubric against teachers by forcing them to remove themselves
from the teaching process as much as possible so the student can
take "charge of their learning." In no way am I contradicting
earlier statements made about the education system: namely,
when I asserted that students are not taught how to think, but
what to think. Principals don't want to create a thinking
classroom--what they want to do is make the teacher as
irrelevant as possible and this is not what I propose. I believe
students should be taught the tools for independent thought so
that they can participate in discussions with their own unique
voice. Administrators and some lawmakers today (e.g.
Bloomberg), put rigid and sterile limits on teacher involvement
in the learning process--not to help the teacher 's pedagogic
performance, or to increase student achievement--but as another
way to punish teachers arbitrarily. And why not? - Education
today is so robotisized that students need not even attend a
physical school location; the justification for schools diminish as
the years go by. Teachers are told not only what to teach by the
state--which, goes against the inherent basis of teaching--but
how to teach, how to stand when you teach, how to circulate the
class when you teach, how the teacher's desk appearance should
look, how the homework collection process should be organized
etc...

Look at the trends in the job market. Do they not become
dumping grounds for those educated by the state? If the futures
of tomorrow are seated in classrooms with teachers who are
employed as academic robots, what becomes of the employees of
tomorrow? Employers increasingly isolate employees in little
cubicles off to themselves limiting the need for socialization
skills. Jeez! We don't even talk on the phone anymore, we text
everything. Lastly, jobs that do return back after the recession
pay so little, require so little brainpower and request mundane
and repetitive task be performed that even a parrot can do. We
need more public aid to revive the lost art of teaching. Happy
teachers practice their ART, instead of regurgitating some old
fossil's view of proper teaching- (i.e. The Danielson's Teaching
Rubric that somehow turned into an evaluation device; just

another example of how certain classes of people profit off of the social experimentation on the masses). Teacher turnover systematically infiltrated the school system especially during the Bloomberg administration when he demanded schools focus on "high stakes testing," and to show results immediately thereby automatically pushing teachers evaluated as "unsatisfactory" into reject enclaves. Not even schools got an exception--if they didn't perform to standards, Bloomberg closed them instead of reforming them (of course so he could justify the increase in charter schools). The people need to know that too many standards impoverish public schools. Once you get teachers hooked on the art of teaching, maybe they might stay longer than one year!

And should we even speak of the violence in the schools? We couldn't at 226M--at least not openly. During one teacher development day, one of the teachers attempted to bring up our schools ranking on the "most dangerous schools list" and was immediately shut down. Assistant Principal Jeanne Bradley scorched the teacher with her eyes, put her palm up to shut the teacher up and she stated: "Our schools are going to always be on that list due to the kind of students we service." And the case was closed. But was it factual?

The violence at the school reached an unprecedented level--for that school year. H----, the only senior teacher remaining taught a really volatile classroom. I must admit I appreciated not having that class. On any day of the week you could hear screaming and chairs thrown across the room and hallway, school equipment breaking, and all other kinds of mayhem. Sometimes I forgot I didn't work at Bellevue Hospital's Psyche Ward. As occurs often in locations with few resources, our students turned to violence as their last ditch efforts to provide a visual that something or someone in this school failed them and like always nobody paid attention or thought it necessary to correct. Only when it passed the line of acceptability did the topic of school violence receive a cursory glance from Shelly.

Coming down from lunch one day, I heard the usual: screaming and yelling and breaking of furniture, but little did I know H---- was being assaulted by one of her students. When I came upon her classroom she wandered out in a daze with a bloody elbow and in a state of shock. Her eyes didn't leave that sarcastic impression as usual. In its place, the look of fear, belittlement, and that look of finality. Her face screamed: I'M DONE. I looked down on her sitting in the hallway up against the wall in a student seat. I kept glancing towards her and then at the classroom, which quietly looked like mayhem, then back to her. My paraprofessionals had lined up my students outside of the classroom as I had taught them from the beginning of the year, and they waited patiently for me to arrive. Walking to my class I couldn't help turning my head to look back at H---- again and again. I looked at my students lined up against the wall and then we all proceeded into the classroom.

I found out later that the administration bared no part of the weight. They never even showed up to the school to see if the situation had subsided. Never did they call her to make sure she didn't suffer any permanent injuries. They would never produce any meetings to inquire how to make the school a safer place. They didn't express the least bit of sadness at possibly losing a veteran teacher? No. The system worked just the way they intended it to. What did they do? They hired another teacher, a teaching fellow, and threw her into the same classroom without any assistance on how to deal with an extremely violent class. She didn't know how to deal either. But if you wanted a job, you "played the game." I saw this as a cycle of teachers in and out of violent, destitute classrooms.

Teachers at 226M "just got by." This may go against common knowledge, but survival is non-productive and a waste of time. I hate when people say, " Another day, another dollar," or "I'm just glad to be alive." But, if you live for nothing, why live?-To just make it? -To just be? - Be gone, please! And, if survival produces nothing of value, what can you purchase with it? -What can you do with it? -Gaze on it like a piece of lifeless meat? People who describe themselves as "just making it" curse themselves and everyone around them. I'd like to think Darwin loaded the sciences with credible theories--For instance, his assertion of the survival of the fittest. But the unfit live on, and on, and on. They are everywhere and in every profession. They wear the teaching profession like a wet blanket. They don't want to be there! Let's redefine "Making it". "Making it," means producing surplus value. Educators who see their students as a potential increase in individual wealth serve as the greatest among their colleagues. Instead, we have these "social instinct" pushers who strive for the "global" everything--the "we are the world types." "We" they say, need to clean up the environment"; we" need to conserve; "we" need to strive to fix the justice system. Justice? Blah! Don't include me in that "we," for one, I refuse to recycle, and two, I see no purpose for educating everybody because knowledge that sits its fat ass on the couch and watches as the world disintegrates into authoritarianism gives me high blood pressure. But, still I can't help it. Apart of me looks back in hope that one day just one day...

We enrich life for everyone when we produce more change in the world in a shorter amount of time than it took the generation before. This book will have advanced society threefold in comparison to any social justice campaign, if not for only simply persuading everyone to take their seats. As the kids say, "Have several seats."

Survival in the teaching profession amounts to a last ditch effort by many teachers to remain loyal to their profession. But, they look so miserable doing it. This need to "just get by" originated out of the bosom of disenchantment. In a 2013 report, "Met Life survey of the American teacher, documented a broader dissatisfaction among educators. The report, which is based on surveys of 1,000 K-12 teachers and 500 K-12 principals, shows a precipitous decline in morale. The percentage of teachers who rated themselves 'very satisfied' has dipped 23 percentage points since 2008, from 62 percent to 39 percent—putting it at the lowest point in 25 years." (htt5) However, those best adapted to teach today are those more concerned with statistics and data and less so with their students social, emotional, and educational growth.

I conceived that I would not allow the evolution in teaching to affect me. From experience and working at PS 226M I've learned that the intensity of the problems you encounter relate directly to the level of respect demanded by you. Where your troubles are, "There you will find your treasure." I'd like to think of my problems as trinkets to wear. Problems emerge like the handbags women wear or the fitted caps that the brothas' sport: as accessories, they make or break the entire outfit. Wear your problems on your sleeve! For those of you just getting by I'm sorry that you can't afford your problems. Think of it like this: go out searching for problems inside, under, outside, and on top of every surface--they are opportunities to decorate oneself with respect.

H— returned to the school one more time in December to collect her belongings. She snuck into the school in order to hurry up and get out so as not to incur the barrage of questioning from nosy staff. That's all everyone seemed to want-- to get out of 226M. Everyone seemed to either wait for the day they made tenure to make a run for it or some other anniversary that emancipated them from their misery. Everyone shared that look; but, she, now having many years of teaching under her sought out that dream in practice and escaped of her own free will.

She made it out, but what about me? A newbie, I just started, and now the only surviving senior teacher resigned. She was my only hope of combating the upcoming winter. My time hedged itself on the horizon. Although my mentor shucked his mentoring duties and the administration left me to my own devices, I knew that claiming ignorance would help the situation little. They couldn't care less that my class suffered on account that they prospered from intentional cycles of starving out new teachers. Evaluations hovered above on the horizon and I felt my time at the school exhausting itself.

CHAPTER 9: Class

I didn't want to "just get by", I took on this job to do a job and I intended to accomplish it. After speaking with other teachers about how lost I felt in the classroom, word germinated and spread among the other teachers until it finally touched Imma's ears. One day in November while on lunch break I rushed in every direction throughout the classroom to get everything in order so that I might eat one bite before lunch abruptly ended. At this point, I recognized my disdain for the school. Lunchtime served as a brief moment to barricade us from our burden and our masters. As I packed up my things, before I knew it, Imma quietly crossed the line on the floor, which separated my classroom from the hallway. Unlike Jeanne, she didn't put on an obvious act. Putting one step in front of the other very cautiously she marched into the classroom with a smile reining in her stone cut face. Up until now, I encountered her only so often, but never unilaterally. She communicated her sweet demeanor with a smile. Originally from Spain, her English beckoned for more schooling. It made me wonder how she got so far in the school system with that poor excuse for English —her lexicon matched that of a cast member from Love and Hip Hop Atlanta. Her face crisscrossed whenever anyone politely asked her to repeat herself. But, she was on the come up. Whenever we had schoolwide meetings, she would stand side by side with Shelly and never was she afraid to cut Shelly off if she wanted to interject.

As she stood in front of me I looked down at her, assaulted by that purple streak in the front of her hair; I stood in awe that she thought it age appropriate. Her face wanted to cry out that it still held onto its youth, but the hardness and lack of youthfulness said she broached the beyond. She said, "Hi, Hey Fredrick," as she always mispronounced my name, at times, purposely. "How's it going?" I held my composure, but I thought to myself are you kidding me? How many weeks lapsed before she or any administrator decided to come in and check on the development of the new teacher? But knowing better, I played down my critique of the school. We made small talk about any and every irrelevant subject under the sun and I despise small talk. It's something about small talk that kills a little part of me each time I'm asked to take part in it. I'm a realist. Tell me what you want, I might do it if not to only get you out of my damn face. Even while watching a movie or reading a book I want to zoom past the narrative just so I can get to the gist of the story. But, her kind often engage in these cordial traditions--not out of any true concern for the person they're speaking with, but out of reconnaissance. She asked if I obtained all of the books for the math program and looked around my class observantly. It looked like she expected someone else to come in and observe as well so she took the first chance she could to get the first look. Her position placed the onus on her to maximize results from the math program. This visit, in retrospect, really benefited her more so than me. She continued "You know what I'm going to do, I'm going to help you; I think you could use help, right?" I couldn't deny the veracity of her statement.

She sat down at the student's table and pulled out a seat for me. I didn't think she intended to help me so soon on my damn lunch break. Looking at the seat for a moment, I hesitantly sat. She saw the common core standards posted on my walls. "Cedric, do you think your students can actually achieve those standards?" I didn't know if she posed a trick question or not so I called her bluff. "No, I don't think they can." She slapped her hand on the long rectangular desk that we sat at, "Then why on earth do you have them posted?" "Because, Shelly said," she interrupted me, "never mind that," she said, I want to make your classroom into a functional place for your students to learn. "Your students learn differently than other students, they're special right, I mean, their bright and aren't they so sweet? -Don't you just love them?" she said, as she twisted her head from side to side and smiled so hard the lines stretched from her eyes to her temples like rays of sunshine. I sat there looking at her choosing my words carefully, I agreed by nodding my head. Finally! I said to myself, someone who knew my struggles and manifested the will to help. My class was nothing but an experiment to me. No other classes as "low" as mine existed in the school, and the other teacher who did teach similar students the previous year seemed like she made it through last year by luck.

As Imma diplomatically put forth her position I came to see a divide between her and Shelly. They used teachers and other staff to advance their own political agendas in the school system. Both did whatever necessary to win. Yet, Imma differed from Shelly in some respects: she showed her true colors to certain staff to try to win them over to her side, thereby undercutting any loyalty to

Shelly; she instilled an immediate fear in the staff whenever she arrived mostly due to her bi-polar tendencies to switch from insanely nice to politely vengeful. "Here," she demanded. "I'm going to give you a tool that's going to show you how to structure your lessons and what to teach. It's called the Beldengreen Reading Assessment. It shows you skills that your students need to learn such as," she opened the assessment and turned the pages. "See, basic. So basic as to require a student only to.... look at letter C she said. "Matches large clear photos to identical objects; matches photo to object for a favored item; matches photos to objects for 2 or 3 favored objects and so on. Most of these skills require the students to learn how to match, the basics of assessing pre-comprehension, pre-reading skills. Cedric, your students cannot read yet so we have to build those pre-reading skills in order to prepare them for reading." She noted again how the common core standards bothered her. I interrupted, "But what about the reading curriculum maps that Jeanne sent out?" Her eyes pierced me getting angrier, "Cedric, forget the curriculum maps, forget the common core standard. I'm helping you. Do you trust me?" I nodded in agreement. "Well, trust me when I say that this will work for your class." I felt her politicking in a way to win me from Shelly and onto her side. I just wanted to come to work and leave and go about my business. She made a big performance like we worked in the Oval office.

Speaking to other teachers after Imma left my class they assured me that Shelly hated the idea of using anything other than proven, evidence based academic tools to teach our students. A dangerous gap in the earth opened up below me pushing my mind in two directions. The next day I came to class ready to implement the new strategies I discussed with Imma.

I came to class the next week armed with new strategies and methods that I thought would also reinvigorate my paraprofessionals. One of my paraprofessionals, Dhar, was an Indian "actor" turned paraprofessional. His dark, graying hair flowed down to his shoulders; some of the teachers used to joke that he got his hair did at the same salon as some of the other female staff. At times he would wave his hair like was auditioning for a Pantene Pro-V commercial. He set himself off from the rest of the paraprofessionals a lot as if he had a separate mission at the school. This stooge complained every step of the way. From the beginning he left wet slime over any and every plan I intended to implement in order to improve the apathetic environment. He hated a younger teacher upstaged him; he hated the teacher he worked under surpassed his educational achievements .He hated everything. Most of all, he despised me for treating him with respect. If I had planted an evil seed he would have had a real reason to hate me.

The first meeting I held with him and my other paraprofessional took place in our classroom. They pulled up two of the student desk as I sat in a chair facing them. A very impromptu meeting, I wanted to explore some of their backgrounds and get to know them, and for them to get to know me. He and my other paraprofessional dug into the trenches and launched their first attack: "In our countries we were both teachers." For all I cared, they could go back to their damn country (but I'm a professional LOL). In addition, it's next to impossible to create change when other stakeholders refuse to get on board. Change never comes easy for those who've survived day to day by living like robots; any change made without reprogramming their understanding causes a total meltdown. I cut in, "I expect this year to be fun for all of us if we can think big and not limit the students in our class--if we have high expectations for them, they have no choice but to succeed." Dhar sat up in his seat to show that he had a voice too, " Well, other teachers have tried and the students never, never seem to get the point. I think all of this academic work is wrong for them. They should be learning basic things, like how to tie their shoes; for instance, M----- can't tie his shoe." I informed him that we had to teach what the school said to teach but that I could find ways to intertwine academic and functional skills--which, I did. After lunch, and during Social Studies, I taught my students how to brush their teeth, a task that benefitted them more than all the Native American studies in the entire world.

But, that wasn't enough for Dhar. As a passive-aggressive form of resistance he upped the ante. Already a lazy bum, he chose to add to this infirmity to his poverty of thought. Many days, while in the middle of teaching, I would catch him sitting behind the students with his eyes closed--at one time he even began to snore. When my other paraprofessional attended to students needs outside of the class, he walked out to go who knows where, and his vegetative ass wouldn't come back for over 20 minutes. At the beginning of the year, I explicitly informed both paraprofessionals that I, as the teacher, should never be left alone in the classroom with another student. That meant nothing to him; he would have loved to hear of something unfortunate happening to the students or me as a way to get back at me. When this emasculated, debauched excuse for a man was conscious, he didn't work. I taught the students during direct instruction then assigned group work where they could practice, over and over, the same skill; and of course they needed help. Where was Dhar?-Either yelling at the students to do it right the first time or in the back making half-hearted attempts to quell his anger and self-hate, which he misdirected at the students. Maybe if his acting skills burned half as passionate as his rage, his career might have carried him away—preferably, far away.

His actions went to show that those below as those above hate to see change. Change requires work; change requires movement; change demands the muscles to awake from a long slumber and stretch forth in pain; change causes pain. It's hard to instruct a class when you have "professional help" who need instruction more than the youth. But employees will fight for the littlest of scraps that includes working hard to make another employee look bad. In truth, all they ever give us is scraps. I don't care if you make 20K a year or 500k—if you find yourself working for another man or woman, face it, you're cursed! You can't put a price on the breath of life. It shows just how small we've become when we think it's normal to get back at our co-workers, men and women in the same degraded status as our own. You can never repay others for the harm you think they inflicted on you. The world keeps turning, and revenge holds you in place. When you "get back" at your coworkers, you attack yourself and your own kind. Why? -Life damned them to the same miserable fate you blaspheme, and few know the way out; and those who do know won't tell the rest of us. I wonder why? When school politics stand before student learning no amount of teamwork will help grow healthy schools. For example, Dhar thirsted for power that kept eluding him. He came from India with hopes of becoming a great actor, one dream squashed; he worked under many teachers half his age, which only squashed his pride. He now worked under a teacher with fresh and innovative ideas, but he remained under and an old rigid, bureaucratic state of mind that prevented him from advancing.

And the higher ups loved this division; it's these contradictions and conflicts between us that provide them their nourishment. At an accidental meeting I had with Shelly, I bemoaned the fact that my female paraprofessional felt compelled to take so much work home because of a lack of time to get the work done. All the other teachers cosigned this: they too had to do their work at home for free. She pressed her lips together as if she was a member of nobility and like the head mistress of a plantation in the 18th century said: "Cedric, she knew what she was in for when she came to work here." She shook her head in the up and down position signaling to me that I should agree with her. She went on, "The children come first," right? And I, I didn't fight her on it.

As the fall turned into winter, Shelly's demeanor froze in a rigid position. For example, according to the law, teachers and staff should come together to decide what's best for the students IEP (Individualized Education Plan), at least that's what the law intended." Each public school child who receives special education and related services must have an Individualized Education Program (IEP). To create an effective IEP, parents, teachers, other school staff and often the student must come together to look closely at the student's unique needs. " However, Shelly exercised her own law, she demanded the teacher draft the IEP and then she would dictate every portion of the document bringing into doubt the teacher's best judgment. I have countless emails where she emailed me back to change specific words and phrases on IEP's; at the beginning of the school year she practically rewrote my IEP's! (see supporting documentation). For the most part she called me when she wanted to make changes in order to prevent a paper trail. Her behavior signaled she believed she stood above the law. She acted like a CEO principle making every effort to cut corners so the school would not have to pay for all the required services demanded by law. She cut corners, but she also until this day cuts the opportunities of disabled students in her school to save a George Washington!

The public school system in New York City composes itself of warring camps: In district 75, primarily, administrators, teachers and paraprofessionals. They wage this fight on many fronts, and both sides have dominated at some point in the school systems history. It's nothing else but class warfare! The war between these two interests is not an easy apple to dice. There exist no good or bad guys, just interest willing to do whatever it takes to fulfill their ambitions, all at the expense of the children. Administrators think they are destined to rule by their granted titles alone; the teachers want to be treated fairly, unfortunately, they refuse to take the risk necessary to achieve what they want. As a result in New York City the children come last. No side will concede. These inherent divisions in schools keep them divided against each other, resolving nothing, and accomplishing significantly less than possible. And "if a house be divided against itself, it cannot stand." For, the division grew from up under teachers to the point that many didn't fully even understand why they hated the administration or why the administration hated them. However, cognizant of the emotional intensity of the moment they didn't have the vocabulary to define it. To recognize the real culprit we must turn our eyes inside out and look at ourselves. But, what's ugly hardly ever wants to gaze at its reflection. The tension between administrators and teachers originated from a natural contradiction; no real culprits existed, just incompatibilities. Teachers teach; administrators do what?

We should outlaw administrations in schools! If you run education like a business, what's the result? Teachers conduct a social good, while administrators accomplish exactly what? -The good for themselves and their careers? We should go back to the old days when teachers taught comprehensively without obstruction. In a real school, teachers orchestrate every facet of the schools operation. Shelly liked the division in the school because it displaced the attention from her; it prevented the teachers and paraprofessionals from uniting against her and her ambitions. Till today that war rages on with no end in sight.

After considering the politics, I accepted what I knew from the start: I must resign to play the cards dealt. At least the players were clear. I would make it as long as I just survived the year; and as long as I did what they said to do, when to do it, and jump as high as they wanted me to.

CHAPTER 10: Sorted Agendas

In January of 2013, the Department of Education (DOE) and the United Federation of Teachers (UFT) failed to agree on a teacher and principle evaluation system by the state imposed deadline. At stake: $450 million dollars in state and federal money. (htt6) According to a New York State Press Release on June 1, 2013:

"In 2009, the New York State Board of Regents launched an ambitious reform agenda focused on the straightforward goal of ensuring all New York State students are prepared for college and career success. The four pillars of that agenda are:

In support of that agenda, in 2010 the Legislature adopted and the Governor signed into law Education Law Section 3012-c, a new law governing teacher and principal evaluations. In recognition of New York's leadership in education reform under Board of Regents Chancellor Tisch, the U.S. Department of Education awarded New York a nearly $700 million Race To The Top grant. Under Governor Cuomo's leadership, the teacher and principal evaluation law was amended in 2012 to ensure greater rigor and effective implementation, including a requirement for the Commissioner to approve all evaluation plans

The New York City Department of Education (NYCDOE) and its bargaining units failed to meet the statutory January 17, 2013 deadline to fully implement standards and procedures for conducting evaluations and as a result did not qualify for an increase in state aid for the 2012-2013 school year. The state budget adopted earlier this year required any district that did not have an APPR plan in place on or before May 29, 2013, would have an evaluation plan imposed on it by the Commissioner after a two-day arbitration proceeding. Based on extensive evidence and the Commissioner's judgment as to the best interest of the students in New York City, on June 1, 2013 the Commissioner imposed standards and procedures necessary to fully implement an APPR plan within the district." (htt7)

As a result of stiff resistance to settling at the middle ground, New York State made the decision for the DOE and UFT and we all know what happens when we leave important decisions to the State. The mutant legislation they created according to New York Sate Education Commissioner John B. King, "Will identify excellence, facilitate high-quality professional development for principles and teachers, and provide each principle with the autonomy to build a strong staff while protecting teachers against arbitrary and capricious actions." The "arbitrary and capricious actions" referred to here can be unearthed by doing a simple Google search online and reading about all the devious plots principles and administrations in New York developed to make the lives of teachers more difficult than it already is. In essence, this legislation served as a default law and showcased just how stubborn and inflexible the DOE and UFT were. It's just another example among an innumerable pile of others that our leaders don't practice what they preach. At the heart of their intentions lives a spitefulness to get over on the other party.

The first victims of the new teacher evaluation system included teachers like me. Not only did the UFT and DOE have a lack of understanding how the new teacher evaluation worked, so did the principles and vice principles administering the evaluation, even more so the administrators in District 75.

I tried to incorporate Shelly's vision into my teaching plan first, but she had no intention of letting me retain any rights to teach the content in my own style. One day in November I stayed late after school, as was becoming the norm. Running into the main office for supplies I ran into Shelly and her Leadership Academy lackey, Jason Foreman. A white male in his upper thirties/lower forties, his uncomfortable disposition made me uncomfortable. At times he had the opportunity to approach some of our students and you could see a clear disconnect between the two. He would stand there in his suit and tie looking down on the students, utilizing vocabulary the students couldn't understand so he could appear smarter than he was. Whenever I approached him--because he never approached me--the color in his face would bleed red and he would talk slow, choosing his words carefully as if he didn't want to drop the wrong word in my presence. And Shelly's presence alone dispersed everyone in the office like the four winds as often occurred whenever she arrived. In the short time that Jason shadowed Shelly he was a ghost within her shadow; I didn't know who he was apart from Shelly and his queer behavior seemed to suggest that he hid within himself the same doubt. He melded and conformed to the rest of the environment, mimicked everything Shelly did and said, and at times his parroting of her made one wonder if he were really mocking her or did he, in fact, have no self-esteem.

Eyeing me as I darted from my classroom to the office making copies for the weeks English, Math, Social Studies, and Writing periods, she folded her hands together while she sat pleased at the spectacle and asked, "How are things going?" Plane-Jane questions like this always act as a vanguard to a more brutal attack on the way. Seeing as I was having problems with the copy machine--a daily occurrence and that's only if the machine had paper, which was often the main problem--the question deserved another question. Are you that dumb bitch? Knowing the answer before she asked, she motioned for me to take a seat. I put out my left hand signaling that I didn't want to take her time and she insisted, mentioning how pleased she was to "help." Before I knew it, I was caught up in her anecdotes about teaching and how she learned to organize herself. I cut her off because I felt myself nodding into a coma. I asked if she would like to see a sample of the readings. Eagerly, she said, "Sure!" This might have seemed like a silly thing to do to many but when you labor for others, your vision will always take a backseat to their vision, so you might as well bring the reality to the surface and face it head on as soon as possible.

As I returned to the office from my classroom with the Reading packet I handed it to her and watched for her reaction. I sat there in the middle of table while she sat at the edge of the table and I waited forever for her reply. Her eyes dimmed. Jason sat behind her waiting in angst to hear her opinion so he could probably jot it down in his notebook like the square he was. The reading, which I copied off of ReadingA-Z.com from the Kindergarten section seemed to insult her taste. She leaned her head to the side and said "okay." The woman couldn't stop fidgeting her fingers together. I could see the blood vessels behind her eyes working overtime to find a politically correct way to describe to herself what I was doing here with a kindergarten reading for 8th and 9th grade students. "Jeanne told me I should go to this website to download readings since the school paid for a subscription," I pushed the words out of my mouth to force her to say something, to say anything. Shelly hated to show dissent in the ranks so I knew she would not talk ill of Jeanne in front of me. Finally after a long uncomfortable silence, she happily manufactured an answer: "So, I see what you're doing, but we want to make the readings age appropriate; you wouldn't want to read kindergarten stories at your students age would you?" I agreed. "This is what you will do, you will modify the readings in a way that is appropriate for students of this age. Yes, that's what you'll do, right?" It amazed me the lengths Shelly drove to get the funds she felt her school so desperately needed--but at what cost? Her investment was on the line, and nobody above her in the Department of Education could ever know what really occurred in the classrooms at 226M.

Her answer only helped to give birth to another paradox: what was her vision of age appropriate and what was mine? Following others never suited me well; some call it an uncooperative attitude; I call it my birthright. The course of nature opposes the idea of following another human being or trying to see through their eyes. I think sometimes the winds turn into tornados and hurricanes just to agitate followers. Other people's eyes are not mine, and what they see is for them and them alone. Any attempt to see behind the ocular ability of another person gives birth to an abortion of authenticity.

Yet, I accorded her for her years of educational experience. For six hours every day I carried with me "age-appropriate material" and sunk deeper into apathy. I knew my students weren't capable of reading the material no matter how much I "modified" it. I would stand in front of the class, using the workshop-model that Shelly was so orgasmically fascinated with, while my students turned their heads looking at anything more visually stimulating than the books I presented to them; and, this could include looking at and through the window at the wall of another side of the building! The wall excited them more than looking at a paper book, which held no meaning for them (paper books, because we had to make the books for the students using paper!). I often wanted to gaze out of the window myself and daydream about where else I could be and how I could spend my time here on earth more economically. It wasn't the poor economic shape of the school that angered me--it was the disapproval of the administration. How could you blame a teacher who held few resources, and who was trying to do the best with what he had?

Imma scheduled an informal observation of my class on November 26. She decided to "help me" by allowing me to choose the time, then she confirmed. "I'll come during your students morning routine," she said. In retrospect, her visit during morning routine in no way could possibly have helped prepare me for the formal evaluation. A morning routine serves only one purpose-teaching a routine: getting the students to put their things away orderly and get ready to go over the calendar, weather, and current events. My formal evaluation with Shelly needed to focus on a hard academic topic (reading, math or writing).

After the informal evaluation, Imma confronted me about the lesson. Although overall not too bad for a first year teacher she looked down on my performance; obviously it wasn't to her satisfaction. Then she wrote on the informal observation write-up: "you had several groups but again the activities were too advanced for the students; this was evident by the large amount of prompts provided by the adults; and, your questions and your language were too advanced for most students levels and the evidence was the lack of correct responses." LOL!!! Um, okay. Let's see. When you teach students the days of the week everyday and they get the answer wrong (even though they have attended your school for three years now, and they still don't know the day of the week) what am I supposed to do? But, then again I envied my students. How free it must feel to not know its Monday or Tuesday or Wednesday, or that it's not 8am or 8pm. Education seeks to put chains on the everlasting and limitless imagination. As I think about it, there is no such thing as Monday or Saturday, or 10am or 10pm! There is only today. And only geniuses like my students knew this.

Although the evaluation didn't go as I planned, I saw for my own self that my teaching practice excelled without either Imma or Shelly. My parents saw it. My parents and my students tested me in ways that a true evaluation should, and I passed with flying colors. Parents wrote and spoke with me about how their children succeeded at finishing my homework assignments with minimal assistance, and that they seemed more interested in actually going to school. One parent, whose child arrived from the Dominican Republic not more than a few months before, thanked me often seeing how her son's English comprehension sprouted forth quickly even surpassing her English. But, none of this mattered to the administration. I had an IEP meeting with one of my parents on Thanksgiving eve. The parent, in tears, expressed how she and the rest of the family lived in a homeless shelter and had access to few resources, even going to bed hungry some nights. She expressed thanks to me and my other female paraprofessional for taking care of not only her daughter's academic well-being, but also her physical and mental well being. As tears filled her eyes, I described how her daughter continued to make progress in my classroom--especially comparing her behavior to the first day she arrived--in which she refused to do anything, including getting up for lunch. Her mother didn't even know that she could operate her communication device--something she only did in my classroom. When she first came to the classroom, she didn't want anyone to get close to her; she would scream for no reason. After only one month, she began participating in class and most importantly to me--laughing and smiling.

When it came time for my Formal Evaluation, formal relationships came apart at the seams. I taught a lesson about biographies. The curriculum map required students to create their own biographies (for the third year In a row) and Shelly put on a big fuss that I should make my own biography to serve as an example. The purpose of the lesson: to identify the date of a biography by matching the dates (even though some of my students couldn't operate a pencil or writing device, nor could some maintain attention long enough to hold a pencil).

Quick Lesson: Biography is an account of someone's life written by someone else. Autobiography is an account of a person's life written by that person I failed to convince the administration that there was no way possible that a student could create his or her own biography—but simple shit like this didn't figure into their calculations!

Shelly and Jason entered my classroom and took two seats in the back. They remained quiet but the amount of space their negative energy encapsulated was more troubling. They sat in judgment like the arm of the law. Shelly held her writing board to her bosom, jotting down notes, eyeing my classroom like a bug inspector, thwarting the rooms harmony, sliding the items on my desk, forming thoughts to litter my career before picking me apart. They sat down and the lesson began. In the middle of the lesson one of the new students kicked me softly against my shinbone under the table and refused to do the work. This student, whom they couched in my class right before my evaluation, held a reputation for extreme violence. Surprisingly enough they thought my classroom suited him best and right before my evaluation. But, Shelly couldn't care less and she would in now way go easy on me for having this new student in my classroom. As I tried to accommodate the students, he began to cry and flail his arms around--seeing he had a sympathetic crowd around watching. Not even allowing me to solve the problem on my own, Shelly stepped in and took control of my class and my student, using what amounted to baby language to try to console the student. His behavior only became worse to the point that he began to throw up on the floor. This was Shelly's escape; she and Jason left the room with the sick student and she ripped me apart of the write up of the evaluation. Did she give me any credit for forewarning her about the student's behavior and medication regime, which was making him sick and irritable? No, instead she wrote in my evaluation, something along the lines, that I shouldn't have forewarned her about what the effects the student's medication had on him because it was an excuse for bad teaching.

Later on Shelly wrote, " Rather than using a negative consequence to engage a student you should utilize strategies that focus on more accessible instruction, as it is possible that lack of attention or refusal to work is due to a lack of understanding of expectations." LMFAO! It sounded like something she read right out of a childhood psychology textbook.

I won't bore anyone with further details of the evaluation, for like Shelly's husband, you just wouldn't be interested (One small fact about me: I can't stand teachers and administrators who dress and act like old educators; we all know you don't get laid at home so you come to work and decide to ejaculate on the rest of us). Shelly rated me "ineffective" on a scale of effective, developing, and ineffective. She wrote:

"The instructional outcomes represented low expectations for your students."

"I also ask that you adhere to advice and guidance provided by the administrative team, which you chose not to follow in the planning of this lesson. Following recommendations will move your practice in the right direction to support student success."

In other words: SINCE YOU DID NOT TEACH WHAT I

WANTED YOU TO TEACH, HOW I WANTED YOU TO TEACH
IT, YOU'RE A BAD TEACHER; YOU CHOSE TO USE YOUR
OWN MIND, AND THAT'S WHY YOUR INEFFECTIVE.

Like Imma insinuated, Shelly knew nothing about teaching low
functioning special students. She practiced special education as
an opsimath. She envisioned them reading and writing
biographies (autobiographies) like they were Mark Twain or
Virginia Woolf so as to impress any visitor to the school
(superintendents), to show that her special students embodied all
the scholastic capabilities as general education students.
Mysteriously, the work that 226M teachers posted on the bulletin
boards appeared more advanced than general education
students. (hmmm?)

All working relations started to reek of the ca-ca that drives
disgruntled employees to piss on their jobs. It didn't matter how
much I worked on their behalf, the amount of hours and the free
time I gave them after school, the sacrifices I made in my
personal life and the effect this inflicted on my mental and
physical health. No, every backbreaking task those turds put on
me I took.

But, the world turned in another direction and reality showed me
something that I knew since my first job at the age of 16: I'm not
a fucking compromiser; I'm a no-shit taking, back talking,
asshole! My most serious offense: belittling myself when I knew
by visceral knowledge that my life accounted for more than
bureaucratic, mind-numbing, automatistic work. And, when they
come to see that you have pulled yourself up out of the cave of
shadows and wiped yourself free of their dogma, then this is
when you become a threat, a nuisance, and a target. I stared at
the wall and saw that all the images I thought were real actually
only represented what was real; they were images created by the
lights of others who joined together out of fear to make one
bright light and give it a name: education. And as I blew out
their incandescent light and looked up at the terra firma, I saw a
new light that blazed all alone just like me—and that's when I
resolved within myself to climb out of that dark hole and take my
rightful place among the ultra mundane. I am so against the idea
of compromise that I have it tattooed on my flesh: "NO
COMPROMISE." I'm aware that when we prolong a
disagreement, the only concession made is the peace. However,

the man who believes he's paid more than the worth of the object he bought endangers everyone around, vexing us with his cantankerous attitude. I could envision myself falling on that land mine if I had followed Shelly and Imma's plan.

I think situations like this, which are common in New York City's Department of (Mis) Education pre-date teacher disenchantment; it's the soil from which so many bad teachers sprout from--once ambitious idealist, now sour apples. Reaching an agreement comes about by one party--the loser--making concessions. You must at all cost get the upper hand on your opponent, that is, steal the advantage--and sometimes just steal. And Shelly and Imma possessed both capacities. It's all they knew; it's all they'll ever know. They corrupted their morals or maybe these were their morals? But, I can't help reforming my opinion of them. Maybe they relapsed. Maybe at one time, just like disgruntled teachers, they too, valued the light in themselves —but maybe that faded out over time?

However, my refusal to submit to their evaluation was a twist of fate when the plan they had for me didn't go as planned: In their design, they intended for me to take the bad evaluations in stride--thinking that guys like myself aimed for low hanging fruits. I was supposed to take my bad evaluations and leave at the end of the year figuring I had no place at the school or no chance of getting tenure with bad evaluations. If I maneuvered correctly, in their minds, and left at the end of the year, the probability of me finding another teaching position would have been 100% in my favor since teachers are allowed to take another position without notifying the principle till August. Plus, many schools hire new teachers before that time. We would both benefit according to the plan. I would remain employed--even if I waited longer for tenure (The ultimate goal of every worker bee!). Shelly would hire another first year teaching fellows (male token teacher) at the lowest pay rate as each previous year with no complaints. The system would work as crafted.

But, the working landscape changed when I complained. I can't help but think that compromise makes for a republican form of governing oneself. And look at me. What the hell do I look like? I'm a ghetto ass aristocrat!

The formal evaluation compounded the informal evaluation

conducted by Imma the month before; as a result, before the end of December I now owned two negative evaluations. I must admit their under-valuation of me bothered me at first. After my own critical appraisal, marking the effect their judgment had on me, I raged for even caring about their uninformed and biased rating of my teaching ability. Both of their ratings about my worth and value as a teacher should have amounted to so little: not only due to their apparent lack of information about how to effectively conduct the evaluations, but if not solely on account of their privileged position. They elicited me as a pawn in their game. I could have taught my ass off and they would have assessed me as no better than ineffective. For in the end, I took inventory of my job and the stock showed that you can't serve two masters--and it's even more improper to serve one! My biggest mistake was not showing them my behind at the job interview.

When the UFT representative at the school saw what was happening, we discussed the evaluations. She made herself available to all of the staff, but I never saw myself needing her assistance and not in the first year. She, remaining cautious of her job and her dueling duty as a Union rep, made for an interesting display of behavior. We couldn't speak on school grounds for one, someone might hear and the spies lined the school, two, it was against contract rules to speak on work time. Even when we stepped outside into the free air, we looked back to ensure nobody could ensnare any part of our conversation. Not only does the school look like a prison, it operates like one too. It's a brick building, with two blue doors in the front, which often remain shut closing the students in. When you first walk in, you have to go to the security desk, where New York City police officers kindly greet you. The whole thing seemed so secret service, intelligence-like. The working people have to meet in secret so as to protect themselves from the heavy handed backstabbing of coworkers and management. She didn't tell me everything I needed to do, but she did inform me of what I shouldn't do, which held more importance in my situation. As a cork in the school systems machine, my situation occurred on a yearly basis. The all female administration harassed the male teacher year after year, often causing the teacher to quit at the end of the school year. I knew she spoke the truth based on the email I received from one of my parents hinting at the frequent turnover at the school. The UFT rep gave me a little advice about watching myself at the school. I cautioned myself from reading

too much into the relationship with the union. But, the counsel
she provided guided me in a more optimistic direction. I also
think this linkage became my downfall for it's the times when
you feel your all alone and nobody comes to your rescue that you
heed the adhortation that life gives you--you discover how strong
you really are. It's a disability to have people you can depend on,
for the unsound opinions of other people counsel you against
your own powerful impulses. The counsel of other people waters
down the potency of your natural intelligence.

CHAPTER 11: Common Core

At the beginning of the school year, New York State and its confidence in the states Common Core Standards--new national academic benchmarks in reading and math--failed to mobilize teachers and parents across the state with the same amount of pride. "What's the big issue?" many people argued, States have been setting standards of their own for a long time:

"Common Core is the conclusion of many years of the expansion of nationwide controls over educational issues, which should for all intent, remain at the local level.... The beginnings of Common Core can be traced to the 2009 Stimulus bill, which gave $4.35 billion to the federal Department of Education which then created the "Race to the Top" competition between states. In order to qualify for funding, the states needed to adopt Common Core sight unseen. An added incentive to adoption of CCS was that participating states would be exempted from many of the more onerous provisions of George Bush's "No child left behind" program." (www1)

"Proponents say the Common Core was designed to ensure that children, no matter where they go to school, are prepared to succeed in college or the workplace upon graduation. Opponents argue that many of the standards are not age-or development-appropriate, and that they constrain the ability of teachers to adjust their teaching to their individual classrooms."((htt8)

In December, before the beginning of the winter recess, Shelly and I crashed into each other at my bulletin board where teachers were required to hang our student work samples. Half of my students suffered from fine motor skill setbacks--meaning that using their hands to manipulate objects such as pencils and scissors posed difficulties, making it next to impossible to write anything intelligible. As a substitute, my students pasted pictures of things they would otherwise write. This made my job ten times more difficult since they depended on me to provide them with vocabulary. If I didn't provide them the vocabulary, they were unable to communicate their needs. As me and Shelly faced off at the bulletin board she complained about my work samples. Her face hung as she gawked at the worksheets disgustingly and asked, "What is this?" I explained, according to the common core standards of kindergartners and pre-k students, this is what their work should look like. She stepped back with her finger still on one of the work samples thinking, as always, of a politically correct response but her patience for me subsided. She couldn't understand why my student's work looked like a kindergarteners. I said, "Imma and Warren (my assigned but absent mentor) told me, at the beginning of the school year, that my student's work should align with kindergarten common core standards." She dispatched a quick disapproval. "Your students work has to align with the 8th grade common core standards," she said. We both stepped back and stared at each other with blank and utter confusion. "But they don't work at an 8th grade level," I responded in a statement-but-question like manner. We went back and forth until at the end of the conversation both of us left perplexed.

Shelly amazed me. It's as if she never encountered an opposition in her lifetime, even a polite form of opposition. To be totally honest I've come up against too many white people (including Jewish people) who feel it's their right and duty as American citizens to ensure that people of color stay in their place. My questions attacked her birthright as a white American to speak without being questioned. But to speak colloquial--I checked that bitch at the start! I'm sorry; I hail from California--not Mississippi! I've lost a lot of opportunities in life for standing my ground; I've been shot down for my color on so many occasions I can't number them--so much that I've come to know the feeling in my heart (those palpitations that beat the whisper of a soft and ancient, no)! This wasn't my first time at the rodeo.

At the age 27 I went on a job interview at a non-profit agency in midtown Manhattan. I did my research on the organization and the position advertised, plus I counted in my educational and working background and came up with a reasonable salary requirement. I placed the salary requirement in my cover letter. When I arrived to interview with the manager, an older Jewish lady who reminded me of so many other Jewish ladies I've encountered in my career in New York City--very, rather, over talkative. (I'm going to be labeled an anti-Semite for even mentioning that she was Jewish, for like racism between whites and blacks, we can't mention the r_____ of Jewish people in the twenty first century's post r_____ America; in all actuality, I like Jewish people a lot actually, and being from California I never really encountered any really religious Jews; but, I can't help but notice some similarities of the ones I've met in the job market in New York City). As soon as the interview commenced, and we drove towards the issue of salary, she leaned back in her chair, moved her red bangs out of her face, and said curtly and concisely: "You are not worth the salary you requested!" Taken aback by her rudeness—and non-factual statement—I shook off the blow. I sat up more erect in my chair, which was difficult as I maintained a military like stature. "I very well am worth that much, and more; I actually broke the salary down a little less than I originally anticipated, but seeing your actions right now, I'm in no way interested for working for your little organization." I stood up, thanked her for her time out of tradition and marched out victoriously. Yet, I would be a liar if I said it didn't hurt me to know that someone felt so superior to me that they thought it okay to belittle me without regard to my humanity or even for the fact that I breathe oxygen just like her, and was an animated, living thing. But, that's what equality or the thought of equality gets you!

One month later, I obtained a position at a similar disability non-profit organization, making more than I requested from that rude hag I interviewed with earlier that month. I've come too far and grown too old at my ripe old age of 33 to turn back from fights like this because I've been bloodied before and it's always worth it. There's no going back. Those who are never challenged are always pushed back into their place when they encounter the likes of someone like Sir Cedric--its because of an unmatched power I hold, one word: No.

The winter break passed and I had more than enough time to think it over. I took a road trip across the American South by myself, out of adventure, the same adventure that took me across the world to places far away like Asia, Europe, and South America and beyond. Locked up in an institution of automatons can drive you crazy. Daring to index me as worthless, I came back with more capacity than ever to veto them. There's nothing like the electricity of the open road to give you clout, to remind you of all of life's charm, return all of the things you lost and gave away so cheaply, to ignite that light in you that faded while you slept. When I returned home in January, I wrote Shelly a strong 'white woman' letter.

I went back over that letter, two, three, four times to rethink the decision to press send. I weighed the consequences would likely not result in my favor, however, in times like these we come to a fork in the road and this fork forces us to adjudicate ourselves in order to reveal the innermost truth about our character. Addressing the common core and curriculum easily led to the real problem, that blatant and deliberate obfuscation rendered mainly by Imma and to some degree Warren, Jason, and Jeanne.

While at it, I decided, once again to have a discussion with Jerry about Dhar's behavior in the classroom. Why not? I was collecting enemies like keepsakes. It's my ruling that each and every parent of a child with disabilities in a District 75 school show up to their child's schools unexpectedly and unannounced. Don't stop by the police booth, don't appeal to the school office to let you see your child—walk right in—but prepare yourself. (PLEASE PAY ATTENTION TO YOUR CHILDREN. NOT EVERYONE WHO TAKES ON THIS JOB IS IN IT FOR THE CHILDREN, BACK TO THE STORY.)

I rested on my bed staring at my computer screen as I combed over that letter one last time before sending it. I thought about taking out the reference to a fearful environment and the milieu it might create. I considered it might be too much and that they might take offense. (LOL!) But, then a more sincere and bold thought intruded: "don't let the bastards get away without mentioning every last iota of their INAPPROPRIATE behavior." It's moments like these that we come to an estranged "common sense," and grow fonder of the truth which says: That the path to self-realization is never easy and its never peaceful, and in the end you very well may find yourself alone; those set apart pollute the ways of the base worker bee to the point that they lose themselves—that is they lose their former selves (the worker bee) and take on a new form that is pure, just, and horribly stringent. It just felt good to put in print form what ignorant people in power positions have done to me since I stepped foot in the public education system: defining me, contextualizing me, and orienting me in a bad light for not living up to their moral equation. My self-respect called this arrangement into question after deciding to deracinate their conception of me. Know this: When you are able to make a decision and love it no matter what the outcome may be, then you have rooted out self-doubt. Never ceasing to be true, when we doubt our reality, doubt guarantees itself as the only reality. From a young age we make conjectures about our existence here on earth, and what we observe-the drudgery of our work assures our reality, no matter if it beats the body to the ground or is intellectually non-stimulating. For example, if all you see is mom and dad coming home from work in a state of rage or depression, the effects dance around you mockingly. Our experiences determine our future potential. And since the source of this disease is the mind, we have to do one important thing: change our minds about ourselves. If anything, with equanimity, we must repent for our self-doubt. We have to stand guard against the opinions of others; build mental and physical forts that are impenetrable. Our disbelief assures our success! For too long many of us have taken to heart the opinions of teachers, principals, managers and supervisors who measured our self-worth as lacking. If we believe we are inferior, our definition of ourselves grants us that certainty. The subconscious mind can cheer our emancipation or lock it in. I'm convicted beyond the possibility of a doubt that Shelly's neurosis was due to overcompensating for something in her past. Whenever in her presence, her actions suggested she was insecure with power. It was as if she was guided by negatively charged feelings about herself that she could not shake.

From a young age, my experience in the labor market proceeded in the direction of blame and punishment: my behavior from the start deemed me unacceptable and in violation of the laws of inferiority. My first job was at Footlocker at Southland Mall in Hayward, California. Having wanted to support myself from a very early age, I thought to work the very moment it was legal. After a friend of my sister hired me, not even two weeks passed before the District Manager visited the store and was on my ass. A tall Caucasian man from somewhere in the bible belt of America, he shelved me as a threat from the first moment and I exhibited the same feeling. He gave me the friendly white greeting--some corny ass anecdote about his first job. I was accustomed to this behavior by white people; based on my years in the school system whenever some politically correct white person wanted to come off as non-threatening they sold you the same type of spirits: a distilled volatility. Our most virulent enemies come armed with a smile. I thought to myself well maybe he might be different; he did make an effort to be cordial. But, his actions spoke differently. He immediately checked my sales record on the floor and it had been revealed to him that I was a lead in sales performances (Not to mention he didn't ask about the other's sales representative's record. How did I know? The manager was a friend of the family). My manager approached me, trying to keep her purpose genial, saying that the District Manager requested that she transfer me to another store if I wanted to keep my job. Apparently, my demeanor could turn off some customers. I looked too "angry." So as a resolution to help me "keep my job," in his prudent opinion, he thought transferring a young black male (and apparently menacing) to Lady's Footlocker might make the old women feel safe and happy! -Of course in the hopes that I might quit. I didn't quit. I believed in myself. And this belief was no performance or something I brought out purposefully. My sales performance continued beyond exemplary. Eventually, I resigned on my own terms. As I gazed at my computer screen, I remembered this part of my life so clearly. I knew this program too well, and at the core, I chipped away at my past to find that trouble would find me soon enough as my experience showed me--I might as well preempt the battle.

I have landed on a stubborn fact: that hard workers get nowhere! I can't help but belabor the point that upward mobility is the ladder to nowhere. If you take a step towards our reality, our current economy is no different from a fairy tale. The author of Jack and The Bean stalk must have scaled the workingman's mind when he wrote: "Ah! you don't know what these beans are," said the man; "if you plant them over-night, by morning they grow right up to the sky. Really?" says Jack; "You don't say so." "Yes, that is so, and if it doesn't turn out to be true you can have your cow back." (htt9) The moral of the story: If a man can lie better than he tells the truth, he gets ahead. But, we as workers are supposed to pull ourselves up by the bootstraps? Ha! In this world, instead of a beanstalk or a ladder, there is an elevator to success and it's called: vice. If we remember the story of Jack and his beanstalk, we remember that Jack pillaged the Giant's home many times before he's caught, in which, he cuts down the beanstalk just in time so as not to be killed by the giant. But Jack ends up killing the Giant as he rushes down the beanstalk to take back his belongings from good ol' Jack. Jack and his mother "live happily ever after," after having committed all kinds of misdeeds. How sweet!

It's when you stop giving a fuck that life surprises you with an interesting side; before that, it's all misery. I might not be stealing gooses and harps--but, if you want to really live, you have to steal back everything cheerful stolen from you the first day your lifelong purgatory began--the day you accursed stepped into the education system and the labor market. This is what the teachers mean when they call you names like "inappropriate": they say this behavior is what's "immoral." You know what I say? My dignity—I'll take that back, thank you! My independence--I'll take that back, thank you! My hope--I'll take that back, thank you! My life--I'll be taking that back too--thank you! Nobody has, nor will they ever, witness a thief like me in all their reprobate lives. I am the first and the last. There isn't a man or woman who is wealthy, excepting an heir of fortunes, that has gotten the riches they have without selling their "goodness" and ideas of "hard work".

I decided to press send.

===============

Hi Shelly,

After our conversation yesterday about the bulletin boards/ common core standards I wanted to expand upon, in greater detail, what I had intimated when I said that 'I had encountered many contradictions since September', which I believe have negatively impacted my evaluation and teaching practice as a new teacher at 226M. The intention of this email is two part: to make known my frustrations and difficulties and to, as a result, get a clear and concrete set of academic expectations from you.

As I had stated before, in my interactions with you, Imma, Warren, and Jason (whom I speak with more so than Jeanne or Aracelis), I have received various information that has been opposed to one other.

1. Common Core:
I was told by Warren to place the 8th grade and Kindergarten common core standards on the bulletin boards. I was also told that although my students are in the 8th/9th grade, that most of them operate cognitively at a Kindergarten/Pre-K or below Pre-K level, depending on the administrator. With these understandings, I was informed by Imma to determine what

skills and activities a Pre-K/ Pre-comprehension student would need to learn. And so, by the work you saw yesterday on the bulletin boards, the students were pasting and cutting out pictures to create a timeline (cutting, pasting, drawing being skills that kids at this cognitive level are mastering). However, as I learned yesterday, you told me that I should be focusing solely on the 8th grade common core standards. (As you will see later in this email, one of my recommendations is that I work more closely with you as opposed to the other administrators, so that issues like this will not arise in the future; this has serious implications when it comes time for formal and informal evaluations.) Nevertheless, I don't think you and I came to a concrete understanding about how my student's work should look. I was saying that I look at the Kindergarten common core standards to get an idea of what my students work should look like---is this correct or incorrect? If incorrect, please help me to better understand.

Earlier In the school year, I made it a point to align my lesson plan objectives with the common core but was informed by Imma that my students needed to learn different skills at their cognitive level--this is why she gave me the Beldengreen reading assessment as a launching pad to determine what my students should be doing with regard to reading. However, I have had quite a difficult time integrating these skills with the common core skills. Which should I use?

When I spoke to Jeanne yesterday, with regard to writing, I was told to infer from my students writing prompt what their next steps should be in terms of writing--this is clear and something Jeanne told us to do at the December 6th PD meetings. However, in prior attempts to make writing IEP goals for my students, I have used the writing continuum as a guide for next steps. Here lies a confusing point for me. Am I suppose to infer from my students work what should be the next steps--as Jeanne stated-- or should I be looking at the writing continuum and determining which skills need to be learned next. This is grey area because when it comes to inferences and interpretations--something that I have struggled with since September--it leaves room for interrogation and intense questioning sessions by administration. I need a clear and direct answer about how I should be developing my students Writing, Reading, Math, and Social Emotional IEP goals so that I can replicate the process in the future.

2. Curriculum expectations

It's my understanding, based on various conversations that I have had with teachers throughout 226M, that teachers interpret the final task of each subject, and from there, determine how that task will look for their students. For me, however, I have been reading the final task for ELA, for example, and trying to get my students to do this task. For example, for Periodicals this month, our students are suppose to do a review of a Movie, write an intro statement of their opinion with supporting details and concluding statement. For my class, in which some of my students have fine motor skills deficiencies, this is unrealistic seeing as a Student such as (STUDENT) can only write his first name clearly. My question is, is it okay to interpret and infer from the final task what my students are able to do and go from there? Or should I attempt to get my students to write something with a pen and pencil? I know we discussed using picture symbols, however, if I were to literally look at the common core standards, it says "write", which is not the same as using picture symbols. So, again, I ask the question, should I be interpreting the final task (and common core) or should I be interpreting what it looks like for my students?

3. Interpretations

If, I as the teacher, am in different circumstances, such as listed above, required to interpret common core standards and curriculums using my knowledge based, then I need more confidence from administration, that what I expect from my students, is the right thing for my students. I get the sense that many times we all interpret things in different ways. If interpretation is okay, then I need for you and the rest of the administration to trust that the decisions I make for my students are the best choices for my students. Oftentimes, in the past 4 months, I have been bombarded with opinions from teachers and administration about what my students work should look like; a good example is our discussion yesterday about the timeline worksheet; we al learn differently (and I'm speaking about us as adults), so we definitely will interpret the best way to teach a new concept differently. However, if this is against your expectations at 226M, then I would like to stay in tune with your expectations. So, I ask, what is your stance on teachers interpreting the common core standards and the curriculum?

4.Evaluations

I expect to deliver to you a rationale in response to my Evaluation results at a later time. But, in the context of this email, I want to say that the above-mentioned contradictions played a tremendous role in the results of my Formal and Informal evaluation. What Imma may have deemed Developing in my informal evaluation, may have been determined by you, in my Formal evaluation, to be ineffective and vice versa.

5. Environment

As a result of the confusion discussed above--without taking any blame from myself for not writing this email beforehand-- I believe that the myriad of opinions that I have been given concerning best practices in teaching--by teachers and administrators--has resulted in me appearing incompetent; when the opposite is the truth. I am highly capable of doing my job, but while I am being assessed using rubrics--these rubrics have all been interpreted in differing and unbalanced ways. In the end, it leads one to feel like they are apart of an environment of fear and intimidation. How is this? Because when one isn't certain and clear on expectations, then a precarious situation develops whereby that person must determine, on their own, the right course of action; however, the opposite course of action may be deemed appropriate by superiors. If, I, as a new teacher am not fully aware of what's expected of me, it places me in a position where I'm constantly subjected to an insecure environment where expectations change daily. I think this is the best way to convey to you how I feel at the moment. I think it also reveals how seriously I take my position and my responsibilities.

I thank you for arranging for me to meet with Brian at 14th street yesterday in order that I might see a classroom similar to Y38. I also received Jason's email yesterday with a request to meet Friday.

In conclusion, I want to present to you some recommendations that I thought might help ameliorate the situation.

1. I should work directly with you and when not working directly with you, I need a clear confirmation from others (e.g. such as Imma, Jason, Warren) that what they tell me to do comes directly from you--and is not their interpretation of your thoughts.

2. I plan to reiterate with you, the things I discuss with other administrators and teachers, in order to ensure that we are all on the same page.

3. Confer with you about future plans I have for my students in order to decrease the likelihood of an unfavorable outcome at the end of the unit.

Please, include any further recommendations you feel might help to make me the best teacher possible.

Thank you,

===========================

CHAPTER 12: The Battle Begins

From: Klainberg Rachelle (75M226)
Sent: Wednesday, January 08, 2014 7:37 PM
To: Hines Cedric
Subject: Re: Teacher Expectations

Thank you for your email, Cedric. I will be out of the office for the day tomorrow, but look forward to us scheduling a time to speak to address your concerns. Let's talk first thing Friday morning to arrange a date and time for this discussion.

Best,

Shelly Klainberg
Principal
P226M

=============================

After speaking with the UFT they connected part of the problem to my mentor, Warren Dugdale--who is required by New York State Law to meet four times per month with me. However, I hardly met with him from October to January except in passing. So, as apart of the resolution process I filed two complaints with Shelly: one; mentor services required that I be paired with a mentor and have a working relationship; two, the evaluations were unfairly conducted due to the previous complaint of no mentor plus the administrations lack of understanding of how to administer the evaluations (in addition, there was advice given by Jason Foreman, the Leadership Academy intern principle, which was given and adhered to in the evaluation).

When Imma found heard about the letter, she ignored me in the hallways and in school, period. I remember the first day I saw her after I sent the letter to Shelly. She kept her head down every time she passed me and kept silent. It was the first time I had seen this big mouth, arrogant lady behave in such a way. She feared I might expose her tactics against Shelly, so she chose to distance herself from me. For someone so vocal it spoke volumes about her insidious ways.

When Shelly found out about the requested meeting with the Union Leader, she had Jason cancel the meeting he had set up for us to go over some more common core information-- information meant to blatantly send me off track like the advice given before. They realized they needed to step back and that their actions were being recorded. She came in my classroom and gave me a letter confirming the meeting with the Union Leader, her behavior even more anxious.

On January 17th, 2013, I, Shelly, and the Union Leader, Priscilla met to discuss the complaints. Shelly held her peace stating that her purpose was "listening" only. After I presented all of my complaints, the meeting adjourned. Her muted face said "I'm going to get you for this" while her demeanor couldn't even compose itself anymore. Shelly experienced bouts of what appeared to be panic attacks; in fact, she appeared as if she thought someone was always about to attack her: stuttering, sweating, moving her hair out of her eyes in spasmodically. On the other hand, the Union Leader came off as amateurish and weak. With a faint voice, it sounded like she was reading from a script and her questions and answers programmed. I'm quite sure Shelly was accustomed to this powerlessness from the Union and had no fear of Priscilla; I think she feared me more than anyone. In my presence, she suffered from phthisical bravery. At the end of the meeting, Shelly stated she would give her replies in writing. I stood up and walked back to my class without speaking another word to either party. Shelly and the Union Rep. remained behind to have small talk.

January 22nd: I met with Shelly, Imma, Jason, and Warren at the main school site on East 15th street to go over the letter I sent earlier that month to Shelly.

The first twenty minutes Shelly tried defending herself against my UFT complaints, even though this meeting did not concern the UFT complaints. I sat at the round table without any representation (as Shelly was staunchly against the UFT being there and the UFT's reluctance to show). All the rest sat around the table asserting their power in numbers and trying to intimidate me. But I've encountered cowards like this many times in my life; actually you will never catch a coward alone; remember, they always roll in packs. Shelly preserved her barricaded personality like the lawyers she mimicked. Her ability to fight down and defend herself against any charge was impressive—she's the type to redefine the meaning of red if she had to. With no limits to her deviousness I'm sure in her career she's caught helpless teachers up in their own words; she's a wordsmith. It takes me back to our meeting at the bulletin board when she tried to redefine the meaning of "write." I informed her some of my students couldn't write because of their fine motor difficulties. She stood there, looked in my eyes, and said. "Cedric, when your students cut and paste pictures they are writing--that's their form of writing." I laughed and stated that I highly doubted it. To piss her off--and to be the ass that I am-- I sent her an email with the definition of write:

1.mark (letters, words, or other symbols) on a surface, typically paper, with a pen, pencil, or similar implement.

If only she had dug in and did her research about me, she would know that she hired a word doctor who was more than capable of contending against her sick conceptions of professionalism. You would think she was the first professional by the way she conducted herself. Yet, she met a professional with something I wish all teachers to hold on to for dear life: a voice. Employers like her thrive off of our reluctance to represent ourselves. She never answered one of my questions. As a wordsmith, she never admitted anything or answered a question with a straight answer; it was easier to talk to my non-verbal students. Warren, weak and speechless as always, sat there like cement spread over with a trowel. He looked like a mix between Mr. Belvedere and Mr. Bean. He said more words in this meeting than he had said to me all year. But, this was my mentor? I imagined his mother must have been into animatronics, for he moved and talked like a marionette. He was a poster child for why nobody should have role models. But, more than enough time has been devoted to that troll.

Imma wavered again on her position. Of course she didn't speak ill of the common core like she had done many times before. She also changed her position once again on the curriculum saying that I should not use the Beldengreen Assessment she gave me. "Cedric, it wasn't my intention for you to use the assessment to drive your instruction, only as a guide," she tried covering her tracks. However, exhibit A:

====================

From: Jardi Inmaculada (75M226)
Sent: Friday, December 13, 2013 8:56 AM
To: Hines Cedric
Subject: RE: Reading and Math Levels

Cedric, this is very good.

Now we need to think how you are going to include these next steps in your lessons.

Good job!

Imma

From: Hines Cedric
Sent: Wednesday, December 11, 2013 11:44 PM
To: Jardi Inmaculada (75M226)
Subject: Reading and Math Levels

Imma,
Here are the Reading and Math levels of my students with current levels and next steps included.

Cedric

====================

Imma ended by saying, "I feel trying to help you backfired against me." I asked her how and why but she refused to answer. After asking, once again, for the hundredth time what evidence based research Shelly proposed I use for low functioning Autistic students, she skirted the answer. She wouldn't say if she agreed with structured teaching or PECS (Picture Exchange Communication Systems--where non verbal students learn to request items). She and Imma framed their opinions on opposite sides of the fence. Although they attempted to show a strong front--Shelly and Imma's differing opinions on how to teach children with Autism on the lower end of the cognitive level revealed its ugly face. Imma looked at Shelly with a hard face lacking any emotion. Even after all this discussion and all the time they prepared for this meeting they still could not come to a settled answer about how I should have set up my class. And, it wasn't that I wanted them to tell me how to set up my class, but if the bridge to success was the evaluation, I didn't intend for them to evaluate me according to their fleeting beliefs. I wanted to know what they expected and they intentionally kept the answer from me so that I would obtain ineffective evaluations and leave the school at the end of the year. Yet, keeping your workforce ignorant is a relic of the past, which is apparently still relevant at 226M. When you maintain an ignorant workforce you keep them in peril; they don't know what to expect so they are always in a permanent state of psychological terror when management arrives. I got nothing! Which is what I'm sure new teachers will continue to get.

The discussion came to an end and Shelly lodged an ominous complaint, "I feel you put us in a difficult position." As I walked out, she gave me two sealed envelopes that included letters denying and refuting both complaints I submitted to the UFT. She even submitted a falsified state report that showed that I met with my mentor, Warren Dugdale, four times per month. I would have had more respect for Shelly and Warren if he at least typed in what we discussed! The document clearly shows the category "topics discussed" as empty. And the only reason they couldn't include what was discussed at these meetings was because the New York state closes the programs after a short period of time. He was too lazy to even cover those simple tracks; but then again, knowing how simple the administration was .he probably didn't think he had to do anything else.

Although we solved nothing whatsoever at that meeting, I figured out something important: there is nothing more important than the respect you have for yourself even, and especially in unraveling times when authorities say you don't deserve any! You can't look around hoping someone will have your back. You must turn yourself inside out and become all heart. These are the days when you must sort out your faith in yourself--these are the days when you will need it more than the air you breathe.

CHAPTER 13: Separate But Equal

After the meeting on January 22nd, I knew what would happen to me-what usually happens in circumstances like this: The employer runs a smear campaign based on the instillation of fear, specifically geared at the rest of the employees so that you don't infect them with self-confidence. This fear causes them to go the other way or face the consequences. Expeditious events like this happen all too often in the work world, yet no reform ever takes place. You would think after so many complaints, local and federal trials, and so much abuse, that the American people would rise up and give a confident dissent. But, life goes on as usual. Men and women go to work and beg for the meager sums they are paid in exchange for their silence and their obedience. Although some teachers and paraprofessionals gave me "props" for standing up to the administration, my sacrifice didn't register with the their analysis of the workplace. So, I would pay for my refusal to submit, alone. My type always pays. People are always waiting for a leader to energize them out of their slumber, but I say and hope that no leader ever comes, let it count as their bounty for a flaccid spirit.

As for myself, I stopped giving fear so much of my energy. I dreaded learning these bad habits from my coworkers. I took from fear it's energy and used it to become even more inappropriate. In a state of alarm I washed myself off in the pool of disobedience. With risk, I enshrined my actions in a revered disobedience and I took all accountability and responsibility for my disapproval of their rules that I felt kept me and my students locked in. Many try to hide behind excuses when they break a rule or a law; I took pride in it. I didn't know that joy could stand on its head.

Let me just say this for those of you who wonder: don't ask us (beat down laborers) contorted questions like why the fuck we don't smile at work—our sneering conscious is cognizant of our torture and your maliciousness and its self-betrayal. The notion that hard work equals good character is the last scion of slave mentalities. Are we getting to the meat of the matter here? As long as pregnant women are required to work up until nine months--which the labor market considers caring and just--I've birthed a new slogan: hard character equals good work. We nurse this stupid notion that hard work equals good character from our history of nationalism. Nations often need a group of idiots to believe anything and everything, which includes serving under the banner of patriotism. Do we not remember what patriotism got us? -Wars and more wars. Maybe if we developed patriotism for working, the people might accept the concept of launching a just war on the labor market?

I decided to take the lead. There were no more power struggles with my paraprofessionals: one grew to actually like me, I think? -As much as a coworker can like you. And Dhar, well he fell into line. Something I learned from those in power is that in order to truly break an individual you need **(Censored).** And on the other side of the coin, another true statement: when you stop giving a fuck the mind draws a parallel between carelessness— better yet, shamelessness--and power. As you stop giving a rat's ass about a job, you are on the way up. It's obstinacy like this that pressured me to send the following letter to the State Of New York.

====================

Candace H. Shyer- Assistant Commissioner
Barbara Williams-Bureau Chief
Steven Katz- Director
Office of State Assessment,
Room 775 EBA
89 Washington Avenue
Albany, NY 12234

Dear NY Office of State Assessment Officials,

My name is Cedric. I worked as a Special Education teacher at PS 226M in New York City, a District 75 school which services 11 schools in Manhattan, serving students with Autism. My class was Y38 this 2013-2014 school year and I had four students. All four of my students took the New York State Alternate Assessment (NYSAA), which was administered by myself and two of my paraprofessionals.

I am moved to write this letter on account of how New York State testing for the severely disabled is administered at PS 226M and most likely other schools around the city: I reluctantly write here that myself, my paraprofessionals, and all other teachers and paraprofessionals at my school were compelled to participate in a system-wide falsification of assessment results by the school administration: Principle, Rachelle Klainberg; Assistant Principles: Imma Jardi, Jeanne Bradley, and Aracelis Pimental; and "Administrator"?, Warren Dugdale. I was unsure of the direction I wanted to go with this letter, whereby I wouldn't implicate myself, but I, no matter how I attempt to rationalize it, am part of the duplicity. A concerted effort was put forth by the school to ensure that everyNYSAA worksheet was believably completed by a student at 226M, when in reality, the true results were concealed by tests which were completed by the teachers and paraprofessionals.

This was my first year teaching in New York City as a NYC Teaching Fellow. I was hired by Klainberg the summer of 2013 as a bright eyed student teacher. As a new student teacher, I soon learned it was my duty--actually, more so I had an obligation as an employee at 226M-- to remain quiet and follow the single minded focus of principle Klainberg: to get all students to 80% on all worksheets-- at any cost; and I, as the teacher and licensed educator in the classroom, was entrusted with the required task of turning my face to the injustices imparted on my students and their families.

Please allow me to give you a glimpse into my classroom: Two of my students have fine motor functionality challenges, which makes writing anything at the least, an uphill battle; three of them have trouble maintaining attention longer than a minute; the current math curriculum is identifying the numbers 1-10 on the number line and recognizing that a number represents a quantity--this is below kindergarten level work; my students are not able to read and three of them are not aware that words have meaning; three of them are non verbal; my students are 13 and 14 year old 8th/9th graders.

When I first administered the baseline and final worksheets I was immediately informed by other teachers and staff that the administration would not be pleased with my honest attempts to test the students the right way: the students had to get 80% or more, according to Klainberg, or she would make the teachers redo the worksheet. As you well know, the alternate assessment for 8th graders test students on their knowledge of 8th grade material (e.g. identify the graph that represents a linear equation; or identify a verb in sentence etc.) My students were not able to do this. As a result, there was not one worksheet free from fraud. All genuine and real worksheets needed to be discarded because the students could not understand the purpose, even when the directions were explained using picture symbols. A part of me wanted to portray the honorable and humble teacher, who would turn in any test results no matter the score; however, with the threat of being fired for the inability to teach students with a pre-kindergarten level of understanding, eighth grade material, the pressure from administration squeezed out any chance at me retaining my integrity as a teacher. So, today, broadcasting everything, I hope I can regain some of that frankness I had when I went into the teaching profession.

While working at 226M, it didn't take long for me to learn that manipulation of test results was routine and that I better "put my hands over the students hand and do the work for them, or else". I had to sit down with AP Pimental on numerous occasions to use information from NYSAA documents to skillfully recreate, what she obviously knew were falsified tasks, and make sure they looked "presentable" for the NYSAA reviewers. Feedback from Klainberg, Dugdale, and Pimental went beyond collegial review and indirectly forced many, if not all, teachers to cheat on student assessments. I still have some of the post it notes they attached to the students worksheets. Conversations with all of the administrators on this matter amounted to no more than a form of intellectual ventriloquism: whereby they dictated how the worksheets should look, and the teachers made it appear as if the students miraculously performed the request. Only question that remains is, who are the real dummies?

It's not hard to prove any of this: test any of the students at my site again; my hypothesis is that not one of them will pass any worksheet given them. And far be it from anyone to blame the teachers--they usually work with unknowns whenever they begin to sample the intellectual level of any of their students. It takes time to find out what students know and don't know, then differentiate the learning package. When their exist an administration that insist on deliberately impeding, at all cost, the efforts of teachers to perform the task set out byNYSAA officials (i.e. not providing any teaching time to instill the required learning in their classrooms), then what can one expect but flawed results. None of the teachers at PS 226M were even given time out of any school day to teach the material required to pass the exams. However, Klainberg required that we continue to teach the schools curriculum, which had nothing whatsoever to do with the test sheets required by NYSAA. For example, my students were learning to locate the numbers 1-10 in the school curriculum but the NYSAA worksheets required them to find a missing variable in a linear equation! We are talking about a student going from a pre-kindergarten level to an 8th grade level math understanding in, supposedly, two weeks! If any administrator walked into our classroom and saw that we were not teaching the schools curriculum, we would be written-up: In this way, administration didn't have to force us directly to cheat on the worksheets, we were compelled indirectly. Pimental would always tell us that these scores were a part of the teachers overall evaluation--leading us to the fearful conclusion that the NYSAA was really about testing the teacher more than the student.

There is not one of my student's final assessment sheets which were not altered by myself or one of my paraprofessionals. NYSAA is a running joke throughout the special education system, not only PS 226M, but also the teaching fellows program and other non-teaching fellow educators in District 75. There isn't any validity to any of the test at 226M.
With this letter, I hope to--if not put a stop to this unethical practice--at least shed light one of many questionable events occurring at the school.

Sincerely,
Cedric H.

==============================

As apart of my semi-rebellion I began giving my students recesses without the administrations approval. When I let my students out on the playground, I observed them the same way you study an animal in the wild. The general education students in the other schools within the building were allowed to leave during lunch and had more opportunities for exchanges with diverse student populations. Our students didn't even have a recess. From 8am-2: 50pm they were locked inside the school.

I could only imagine what was going through their minds at the moment. I think seeing them free from the usual restraints in an open and free element discomforted me more so than the students. I didn't know what they would do, would they run and try to get away from the school grounds. It's almost as if they didn't know what to do. They didn't know if was playing a trick on them.

You should have seen the kids run out on the playground the first time I took them out. If you've ever seen a dog hold his bladder for an extended time before he's let outside to relieve himself-- think bigger. At first, they looked back at me and their eyes seesawed between carelessness and approval--I hated that I had to give it to them. For, I wanted them to feel free to appropriate their own happiness without approval. When a human being is set free he must be given his freedom step by step, piecemeal, as he is prepared for it, and only he knows when the time has come for the next step. It's when he demands it!

You should have seen their smiles. I beamed as they escaped out into the endless sunshine that frigid day. Their peculiar shame appeared not to interrupt the joy. The laughter, the laughter charted a new course for them—they would expect this again. I felt the pulse of their life circumscribed by that playground. It could have gone on forever. Their joy gave homage to my joy. And I didn't ask for anything else from them except that they trawled for it for themselves in the future and know that it belonged to them, rightfully—as a human being and as--a living-- human being. I wanted to show them that the world the administration showed them was a lie and that if they would snatch for it that they could reinvent their world. The events that most unnerve us also precipitate our pleasure. It's the sense that with enough courage and boldness we can vellicate fear. And if you can unsettle your fear, you can most assuredly pluck it out! It's a call of action. One, that each and every one of us must search for uninhibited by what others might say or think if we are to complete ourselves. No amount of wealth or intellect can bestow upon another man the gift of freedom. In this minor resistance, the organs within me shifted, especially my heart. The rhythmic contractions of refusal and dilation of freedom opposed the normal school day and everything I had witnessed at the school since the beginning of the school year.

The end of the period prohibited any more outside time, and like that, the light around them weakened. Not one of them wanted to return to the brick building that seemed to trap them in more than the heat. At that juncture I came to the obvious conclusion that happiness was free and it didn't come inside an envelope on a piece of rectangular paper with a dollar sign on it.

General education students on the playground drifted into a state of surprise when my students ran through the playground gates. Surveying their behavior, I outlined that they didn't know how to play with special students on account of the fractured school system that set them apart. The separation between their worlds held them in places they didn't want to belong to. One of my students reached for a ball that had bounced in his direction from one of the little boys playing on the playground. I saw their eyes meet .My student bounced the ball until he saw the other student approach; he wanted to play. The other student's courage fumbled; he didn't know how to respond. So, he grabbed the ball, turned, and walked away back to his group of friends without saying a word. The invitation my student put forth had been sent back to him unopened and unappreciated. Every child who is considered different remembers that moment when they realize they are different. My student's special qualities couldn't break the bounds of bigotry.

I remembered the day I found out I was different. Out on the playground, all of the students ran around playing tetherball, basketball, tag and everything in between. I was in the first grade. A little white girl freely ran up to me, out of nowhere it seemed, and said, "You have big lips," and she extended the "ig" out. As I think about it today, it never occurred to me to run up to her to tell her she had no lips, nor would it ever have. In an instant, like the birth of a baby, or the death of someone you love —my life changed. Before-- I was nothing and everything; afterwards-- I was defined and limited. I didn't know the meaning behind her statement; I just felt deep inside it didn't come from a good place. When I told my mother she said something along the lines of, "and they look good on you." To reiterate, this is all learned behavior.

And the separation of the special students from the general education students harmed them both. Both were missing out on opportunities of learning. What did they learn instead?-To fear the" other". Children learn false realities from ill developed policies at schools. As a put on, they indirectly learn that certain populations are naturally separated from each other, when in reality its man made policies that create these divisions. My students ate lunch at a different time than the other schools (with 6 schools in one building). They ate only among other Autistic children, which sort of defeated the purpose of treating a disability involving anti-social behavior, no? My students received no recess breaks. My student's exposure to general education students was limited to the beginning of school, walking in the school, walking in the hallway, going to gym, going to the library, and going home. In this way, the students indirectly learned that their realities would always be protected from the masses of other students. It gave the impression that each class of students will always face diametrically opposed directions for the rest of their life. And most importantly, that this arrangement was unfixable. However, the answer is more, not less, education; education geared towards human realities instead of dogmatically programmed, moral based ideologies. The school separated the general education students from the disabled students for fear that the latter might make fun of the former, and that the former were so fragile. A huge mistake disillusions the school system: that more general education students suffer from the effects of bullying and low self esteem compared to Autistic students--who for the most part usually couldn't care less what another student has to say about them (most of my students were barely aware that their was a classmate next to them). It's that "do-good" mentality that tries to protect students from their reality: which is, that life is hard and people will treat you badly if you're doing bad or good, if they like or dislike you. We should add a class like this to the 3R-reading, writing, arithmetic--and hater-fucker-ation! It's a fact of life. We can start by first teaching school administrators, then younger general education kids, to treat Autistic students the same way they treat their general education counterparts. Autistic students will not break if you talk or touch them. If you laugh at them, so be it, they are probably laughing at you too!

CHAPTER 14: Teaching

"In 1975, Public Law 94-142 was established by the Congress. That law required that all children be educated in "the least restrictive environment." It was, essentially, the "special education" law. Out of that law comes the idea of "mainstreaming." "Mainstreaming," means nothing more than moving a child out of both special education self-contained classrooms and pullout programs and putting him/her in a "regular" classroom -- in the "mainstream" of schooling. (Regular classrooms are considered to be the mainstream.) But, this interpretation of the law works from the idea that the individual child may be better served by not placing him or her in regular classrooms, that some children are better able to learn in more sheltered environments, such as self-contained classrooms. All children who receive this service do so on the basis of both a battery of tests and conferences with educators, psychometrics and parents, which result in an Individual Education Plan (IEP) for the child. These people decide to what extent the child will be in regular classrooms, pull-out programs, and/or self-contained classrooms (parents have absolute veto power)."(htt10)

Truthfully, neither the administration nor many of the parents were in favor of truly enforcing this law: for one, parents receive all kind of benefits for having their child in such programs; secondly, the school received funding for having a high enrollment. Bingo! You have financial incentives that take precedent over the future of the child. What if the child no longer needs special education services?-Are there advocates there to push for the student to be mainstreamed? At 226M, you could risk your job for attempting to refer a student for a less restrictive environment.

For me, I knew the end was near so I wanted to make as much of an impact as I could with my students. Mainly, I wanted to dissolve their dependence on the paraprofessionals and myself. The shabby ass New York Department of Education thought they were doing our students a favor by establishing a "special school" for them; but, they are hypocrites in that they constantly advocate that special education is not a "location" where students are placed but a "service." I say special education in a District 75 school like PS226M is a disservice! The students are isolated. They never come into contact with general education students and don't give me that crap about the least restrictive environment for even students with the most needs should have exposure to the general population: this is part and parcel of a good education. They should come into contact with students of different cultures, ethnicities, genders, intellectual capabilities, etc. New York City should be ashamed of itself.

I gave my students as much freedom as could be had in a restrictive environment. It was scary at first; I didn't know what they would do. I was shocked at the results, because at bottom, I think most people (young or old) enjoy slaving for others (e.g., Love, Work). I thought the class might turn into mayhem and it did at first. Whenever you have a group of people who heel to their basic right to exist on their own terms it's going to very well seem like they are acting like animals. But, they are just stretching muscles that have long atrophied and grown old: such as their brain. For example, students who are taught to ask for everything. To some, this sounds like I'm advocating for a madhouse. But, we don't know the damage we inflict on young learners when we limit their capability to operate on their own behalf, without asking--asking leads to basic behavior and ultimately, a basic person: accepting and being thankful for the little that you receive--that's what the masses do. I wanted my students to take what they wanted!

After the initial shock I realized my plan worked for some. My most troublesome student at the beginning of the year now took the role of my best ally. I miss him. Distinguished by his erratic attitude, he began the school year throwing everything off the cabinets and counters, including everything on my desk. After he swept all of my papers on the floor, he would turn and look at me to discern my reaction, which I never fed into. After a while, boredom edged its way in and he stopped throwing things on the floor. When I put all of his energy to productive use, I charged him with instructing the Morning Meeting each day. I gave him the teacher's ruler, which I liked to carry although it was old-schoolish. He would carry it and I would notice, unlike when he didn't have the ruler, his chin divorced his chest and lifted towards the sky. There were days when other staff would walk into the classroom and see him holding the ruler and look at me like I was crazy. But, I wanted my students heads in the sky. Former educators were either too strict or lazy, since he seemed dependent on waiting for everything to be done for him and it angered him to have to ask. But, he was reaching the age of 14 and it was despicable. In my short time at 226M, I learned that scraping rock bottom is what public education is about in New York City. This is my disgust.

Other students still needed more direction. When we lined up for lunch, one of my students still insisted on holding my hand-- something I strongly discouraged, but he just couldn't break that habit. As idealistic as I may be, our reality is that many will be pre-programmed to obey. Did I want my students to be disobedient?-No, not yet. I wanted them to learn what obedience was so that they knew why to advocate a disobedient lifestyle. There's a fine difference. Dhar, my paraprofessional, was not convinced of their abilities as I and the other paraprofessional. I honestly think its because he couldn't handle responsibility. How could I expect him to believe in our students when he didn't believe in himself! By this time, I treated him like another unruly child in the class. I operated the class despite him. He just reeked of helplessness. My students would sometimes hit him for no apparent reason and I thought, good—hurt him bad next time.

Occurrences like this brought me to the understanding that the majority of people have within them a pre-disposition to just be. The absolute majority of them will produce nothing of value. They know no other way nor will they ever learn anything else besides reacting to perceived hurts and joys in their lives. This sounds horrible, and many will say it's good omen that I'm not a teacher anymore. However, let's be honest. Many will not fight back against their sorry situation. Sorry students turn into sorry adults! I'm not talking about students who fail classes or students who have encounters with the law. I'm talking about students who just follow the program, work under the radar, and "play the game." I can't stand people who "play the game"--they are the sorriest bunch of.... The summation here is: they are a waste of space. I hate the game. I seek at every turn to destroy it or at least trouble it-and then create my own. Maybe this is why I didn't have many friends when I was younger? Maybe this is why I don't have many friends now? Maybe I'm just a horrible person?

Say what you will, but the class functioned. No longer did I instruct every part of the day and what to do; they knew what to do and I have to give credit to that old Barbastelle, Imma, for some of this learning because unknowingly she reignited my rebellious beginnings—that doesn't mean that the purple strip in her hair is condonable. As the students learned the routines of the class they became more comfortable with their surroundings, which is good for students with Autism. But, thinking more deeply about it, I don't know how I felt about them becoming accustomed to a certain environment and routine when life was anything but routine. I know many Autism advocates cheer for this type of arrangement, but what the hell are we teaching students when we sell them fairy tales that life will go as planned? It's a grave mistake in my book. I liked to throw challenges in my student's way to disrupt them if not to give me a laugh: there is nothing special about a mind that accustoms itself to routine--it can be measured by a cyclometer it's so predictable.

The free environment fosters advancement for the neophyte. I liked the fact that my students walked the hallways among other students--who were bat shit crazy--and still contained their composure and peace of mind among all the mayhem. They coined a new form of self-control that no other class possessed. That's all that matters, at bottom, is the self. It reinforces my semi-veiled thought that freedom is for the few not the many.

Shelly, Imma, Jeanne, they all deserved to rule PS 226M the way they did. Who will outbalance them?-Or who will rein in their belligerence? Who will speak up?

Nobody!

CHAPTER 15: Civil Disobedience

Well. The school tolerated my civil disobedience for only so long.

The meeting on January 22nd solved nothing whatsoever and was strategically accompanied by a letter from Shelly entitled "Intervention Plan"--as if they had saw problems in my teaching that warranted an intervention when I called the meeting into order and with it, their duplicitous actions. Even after the meeting, where we set up a plan for my mentor and I to meet on a weekly basis (remember, according the mentor we had already been meeting weekly). Warren still defied the "intervention plan" and I emailed Shelly informing her that the plan didn't move us any further forward. Thinking that I would let the deadline in the letter pass, both of them thought to accuse me of not adhering to the plan. However, I emailed Shelly first, and my preemptive move angered her. Then the pettiness began.

On January 27th, I emailed Shelly, again, to ask for evidence-based research--a question posed at the January 22nd meeting where she refused to confirm if she agreed or disagreed with structured teaching for Autistic students. I think she didn't want to take a position because she had future plans that included being more than a principal or even a superintendent. So, to keep me from asking again she referred me to a website at North Carolina university that specialized in structured teaching. So, now she agreed with structured teaching as evidence based research approach to teaching students with Autism? Or, was it that she didn't want to go on the record of not supporting structured teaching? Either way, she left me out in the cold once again about what the school's philosophy entailed. I don't think any new teachers ever cared or thought to ask. The trait that made Shelly look like a buffoon is that she could never stand her ground, come out, and answer a question directly. (Political trickery can only get you so far before someone blows your cover.)

On January 29th, 2013 I emailed Jerry Stegman, the unit coordinator and informed him that the automated telephone system did not work for me when I needed to call out of work. Suddenly, in February after all that had occurred, my attendance became a problem. Now, Shelly began reaching for anything she could and she didn't have anything. This is what managers do when they want to build a case to denigrate your character, and as a result, fire you.

The weekend of February 7th-9th I developed unit plans for Social Studies, Reading, Writing, and Math that stretched out for the next month. I was extremely proud of myself for accomplishing something that most new teachers struggle with. With all of the responsibilities of a teacher, it's difficult to design one month of lesson plans. I used the UBD (understanding by design) framework, which Shelly advocated for and that Peter Schmidt taught me over the summer at PACE. My English, Writing and Social Studies units intertwined so as to make the learning even more purposeful. For the second time in the same school year, the school required we teach the Industrial Revolution this time dealing with inventions. I'm quite sure since the school recycled the same topics over and over again that the students had for sure picked up on the definition of the railroad, so I did the foolish thing and attempted to expand their knowledge base. The whole matter was foolish in the first place since the common core standards and the curriculum for the students combined to make learning so inappropriate as to warrant a psychosocial exam for the administration, the DOE, and the State of New York. I decided that if they forced my students to consume this topic one more time then I would at least engage them. I developed a unit plan about investigations as the common core standards called for: "Citing several pieces of textual evidence and draw inferences; read and comprehend non fictional literary text; acquire and use verbs; write arguments to support claims; write informative text; and participate in discussions, building on others ideas and express ones own". What kind of insulting shit was this? Most of my students were not only non-verbal but also couldn't hold a pencil confidently yet, but also they were tasked with "participating in discussions" and "writing arguments?" Yet, I found a way to make the topic somewhat fun and engaging. Instead of rambling on about railroads one more time—can I say, even I hated the industrial revolution in school--I decided to focus on the influx of people from rural life to cities and the corresponding increasing violence that accompanied this mass movement, highlighting London as a place of study. I employed the case of Jack the Ripper as a catch to intrigue the students so that they wouldn't notice, or wouldn't care, that they were actually learning--thereby disentangling that myth that learning need be boring. I anticipated exploring new inventions in crime-fighting such as the fingerprint, linking crime-fighting advances in technology to crime. I introduced the Forensic Science piece during Social Studies first, then Warren came in to analyze my next class, which was Reading, where I introduced the Jack the Ripper Case Study. As he took his post in the back, we exchanged eye contact like two lancers tapping their swords together. I asked Warren to come in and view my class. I was excited about what I had created and thought he would share my feelings. Seeing how far I had come as a teacher since September, I didn't think twice about inviting him. When he entered the class everything seemed normal. He was the same Warren I would see in the hallway with his poor stature, and somewhat lowered head and pride. I feel as if he contemplated suicide everyday he entered those halls. You wanted to reach out and grab him and tell him it would be okay. As he started to pop up more often after our meeting with Shelly, I began to notice that he was just another poor educator suffering from the workplace. He sat down in the back of the class with his notebook as I handed out the teacher made workbooks to the students. I prepared the smart board, corrected behaviors, and began the lesson. It operated as an introductory class so I lightly brought the subject matter before the students and asked them a few simple questions to gauge understanding--in which they understood the subject--then the class ended. I had a math class next, which Warren didn't stay to watch.

Lunch was odd that day: Usually, only two or three of us teachers ate lunch in the classroom together. That day, all the teachers plus one of the paraprofessionals sat in. My lunch was doing backflips in my stomach and my instincts were leaping back and forth. I just felt like something was wrong in the universe--I usually had these feelings right before something bad was about to happen and I've grown to trust them; call me a psychic or a psycho.

As I listened to another teacher talk about her new apartment and her boyfriend whom she enjoyed treating like shit, I kept looking over my shoulder because another teacher kept walking behind me and I hate when people stand behind me. I continued to unexpectedly toss my head over my shoulder to see what she was doing, but I could never catch her in time. After a few minutes everyone disappeared and only the one paraprofessional and I remained. As I finished off my pineapples, I spontaneously asked her a question: "do you ever feel like some people in this school are snakes?" "What do you mean? She replied. "Taking information we speak about, here in the teachers lunch spot, and reporting back to administration?", I asked. She gave me a somber and understanding look and mumbled a few words as she scraped the last few remnants of her lunch out of the crate, relating that," I just mind my business, that's all I know." I nodded my head.

At 12:16 lunch ended and it was time to pick the kids up in the lunchroom. I pulled the door open and in front of me stood Imma and Warren; of course Warren stood a notch behind Imma. "Fredrick, you need to come with us," she said. I raised my index finger up and said, "for the last time, I told you what my name is, my name is Cedric!" If your lucky enough, you reach a point in your life, after all the compartments in your mental gallery have been laid bare, that you fully come into yourself and can't nobody, I mean not even your own mother, stand in your way. Fear is an illusion. As I stood there still with my finger pointed at her, I put my hand down and marched beside Imma into the same office she and Shelly interviewed me in. I closed the door behind me, and both of them stood silent on the other side of the dingy round table that served as the interview room. As I saw Warren, another educator, standing next to Imma, an administrator, the skewed battle lines were drawn. "You're being removed, Cedric. Immediately. We found your book" Imma darted the words out of her mouth. She folded her hands when she said it and tilted her head to the right as If she got the final shot. She had waited for this day from the very moment she found out about the letter to Shelly. I shot back, "that's fine." I grinned at the both of them and I said I would get my things. Expecting this at some time already, I wasn't shocked but I was shocked at the same time. The way they chose to pull the trigger was so wrong, just wrong. But, there are no rules in war and that's something I've somewhat known from the very beginning of my scholastic career--but, it wasn't until that moment that the saying became apart of me. Really, a booklet got me removed from my class? I've seen and witnessed all kinds of corruption back in my home state of California, and the culprits there are smart enough at making a good case for termination; these idiots left crumbs all over the place like the dingy rats they were. It really surprised me how amateurish they were at their deceit. I think that angered me most. I felt like arranging a class entitled

"How to be corrupt in a sophisticated way". Then, my firing could have taken on a dignified tone. The DOE must have trained these dingbats! Imma said, "Shelly will be waiting for you downtown at East 15th Street." Warren said nothing--I'm sure he was pissing in his pants. Had it been two thousand years ago, and I lived in Jerusalem, I would have received a kiss on the cheek. Damnit, Socrates received more justice than I did! But let it continue to be said, "Let him that would move the world first move himself."

I pushed myself across the hallway to my classroom and packed my belongings and exited the building. Imma followed me from my classroom, through the hallway, and through the swinging doors on the third floor and she was about to follow me down the stairs until I told her she was harassing me. But, touche'. She had won that fight and she deserved to gloat.

As I descended down to the bottom floor I spoke with someone at the school who had witnessed what happened at lunch. This person said, "Dhar was going back and forth between the administrative office where Imma and Warren were located and your classroom, and the last time he came out, he had a booklet in his hand; then when he came out of the administrative office for the last time, he didn't have it any longer." Presumably he took the Forensic Science and Jack the Ripper booklets and gave it to Imma and Warren. I figured he would get me back somehow, someway. People like myself don't last long among the obedient. And if I believed, I would have thanked god. I couldn't care less for myself at that moment--and then I thought of my students under his authority and I cringed.

I called the main office. I wanted to see if this was a disciplinary issue or something else; but I knew the answer. Angela, the payroll secretary, answered the phone. "I'm calling for Shelly, this is Cedric from the JREC site." She stuttered, "Oh, Um, Shelly had an emergency and isn't available to answer the phone." "Then when will she be available because she summoned me downtown to 15th Street?" I said. "Uhh, all I know is she is an emergency situation, hold on", she said. She returned and in a hurried voice said, " Okay, you probably should just come downtown and wait for her." I spoke slowly and condescendingly, "How is it possible that she's not there when she just summoned me downtown?" This tit for tat conversation continued for 45 minutes until finally, at the advice of the UFT, I went downtown to prevent being charged with insubordination.

Arriving at the main office sometime between 115 and 200pm, I
sat until almost 2:50, which was the end of the school day. At
that time, Shelly crept out from behind the cubicle in her office
with a letter in her hand. Obviously, she was hiding in the back
on the phone with the Superintendent Designee, Susan
Holtzman getting their story together to speed up the firing
process. From my experience, principals and superintendents
have always been in cahoots. In an almost clandestine way,
Shelly handed me a letter and told me that she arranged a
meeting at the district office at 400 First Ave. in Manhattan. The
heading ironically said" Due Process" and the meeting time,
place, with whom and the reason: "Professional Misconduct." I
loved the "professional" in front of the "misconduct," it made me
sound way more sophisticated than the rats and roaches that
worked under her. She unknowingly commemorated my
disobedience.

I refuse; I refuse outright to keep hanging on to the supposed
sense of justice in this school, this city, this state, or this country.
The form of lynching they chose for me strangled me with extra-
legal, informal, unfair treatment, organized by those who suffer
from averageness!-And don't we outliers always come under
their threat? But the sense of fairness always gets us in trouble.
When we finally understand that there is no justice, and that life
never promised any fairness—life loosens its noose and learns to
tolerate us. I'd rather be burned or hung than go back to
believing that the job place would be anything fair for someone
like myself. I've grown too dark for this world. It's this type of
thinking that set me free--not the sheet Shelly gave me. When
have we ever expected fair treatment and ever got anything
except the other side of the coin? No matter if we did the said
offense or not, they come for us anyway and anytime they want. I
sometimes think back to when I arrived at East 15th street that
day. When I showed up, I stopped at the security desk and was
informed by one of the two black officers at the post that he was
"Told to walk me up." A surprised--but not so surprised--look on
my face appeared. I had never insinuated any act of violence
towards anyone, never had I raised my voice or showed any sign
of belligerence towards anyone at the school (Many experiences
in the past had taught me how to work with white people, mostly
due to the fact that they look for any signs of emotions in black

people to accuse us of being anything but human.)On the way up the stairs the officer said something I'll never forget and in a way that only the two of us could understand: "this is the first time I've had to escort a teacher upstairs," he said staring down as we climbed each step. I was about to understand why.

Due process should be thought of as a nice form of punishment. In today's "civilized" world, we don't send you straight to the executioner anymore. Your torture extends itself as you are, now in the civilized world, required to meet with the government social workers (e.g., lawyers, police, bailiff, bounty hunter) talks to you first--then they execute you. You go through all these processes that give the impression that the justice system is alive, when it never inhaled one breath of life. My punishment was clear: I refused to obey my master and now I would be dispossessed. I expected unequal treatment and nothing else, for those in authority look at "us" as if "we" are deserving of nothing else. And with this realization, I released the noose from around my neck and old Cedric gave up the ghost.

Cannot a sheet scare me!

CHAPTER 16: Back in The Principal's Office

The most defiant of us sometimes have doubts and I met a few on the way to Shelly's office and after leaving.

Am I really a danger to kids? I know my beliefs and thoughts swim in unorthodox waters but never have they destroyed anyone's life. No, if anything my beliefs provided a watering of the human spirit. It's the education system and the labor market (the same system), which destroy us. No matter how many degrees I obtain, and no matter how far up the ladder of success I climb, I'll always own a peril like none other: I'm a nigga. I don't care how much I smile the "white woman smile," or how calm and unassuming I tried to remake myself these past twenty years of my life. I've always been a threat to American society. I've put on white button up shirts, slacks, suspenders, and ties—clothing as stiff as its originators. I've tried lightening the base in my voice a little; I've tried walking with my head not so far up in the sky. I've tried walking without the black man's limp. I've tried engaging in intellectual debate without being labeled "emotional." I've tried.

Here I was back in the principal's office once again. I removed the blinders from my eyes and have seen the light: It don't matter if I have degrees or felony charges—I'll still keep coming up against some white man in "authority" telling me that my mother birthed an existential bastard. And yet, I'm a problem to be solved in the eyes of the teacher, so too the employer. I function knowing that they don't like when you hold your head too high. I see the agency of their heart and mind by the way their eyes gaze downward in the sight of my own--even when I don't intend to intimidate; the fire inside won't let me let them forget. It's the stiffness in my neck that's reminiscent of the tall bridges my people built from self-contempt to love. They hate me because--they love me.

As soon as you free yourself from the axle of the system, its wheels eat you up. Many of us don't even think we deserve more. We spend our entire lives jumping from job to job with the hope of improvement: insanity. For those of us who know better, we eventually become over skilled and overqualified in solipsism to the point that we are of no use in the labor market. At this point, it's either be exploited or exploit. And what's the value of pride when you have no place to rest your head. I get so tired at times. I'd like to pull over and rest at times but there is no place for authenticity in the public arena. I am mortified by my former allegiance to this system. I've learned employers don't hire queen bees--they hire worker bees. But, at this point in my career, the regard for my own well being usurped the ability to survive and pay bills. Now it's different: Waking up to the beat of my heart instead of the drum of an alarm clock--that's what starts my day, now. Laying down to contemplate the day that past instead of the day to come--that ends my day, now. My life is more than wages.

When I think of the school system it reminds me of inner city violence and the ways in which the justice system always works in opposition to each of us. But, even this is old talk and nothing new. We've heard about topics of systemic inequality for so long and still its present. As the descendants of those who have worked under poor working conditions, we still fall under the hand of the slave master thereby continuing the legacy of human exploitation. What has really changed, I ask again?-And think not that I'm referring to the black race--we are concerned here with one group and one group only-- the working class. Working together entails ending this cycle of exploitation. But, I know that will never occur for the state of human nature is evil at heart. Our self-hating condition struggles to change but fails at every push. I've reached the conclusion that humans are essentially the most wretched animals on the earth. They run counter to nature so much that they almost come off as unnatural. Almost. It's only their disproportionate impact on the earth that makes their humaneness stand out--that is, our ability to fuck a whole planet up—I mean, look at the environmental footprint corporations and governments around the world leave today. For generations, many others have written, fought, and died making changes for equality--and what has that got us, really? Equality generates different faces of exploitation and passes them off as civil. We wont ever come together as long as we consider workplace dehumanization and exploitation as normal. Think of education in New York City. The leaders of the educational system intentionally broke the system so that it would function dysfunctionally. Every couple of years the people elect new Mayors and representatives who can finally "fix the system." LOL! They degrade schools in NYC on purpose so as to promote charter schools as an alternative thereby placing education under the leadership of money. Here, even in the heart of academia we uncover the workings of the labor market and its hunt for the working classes everywhere. When the system doesn't work or doesn't appear to work what you fail to realize is that it is, indeed, working: we literally maintain a permanent underclass of students. And so the wheels of inequality and exploitation turn.

When I arrived in lower Manhattan at the Manhattan Borough office, the air was light and I was floating on my determination. At the UFT, I met with a kind lady named Analia Gerald, who leads the District 75 unit of the UFT. A dark haired, kind, but sturdy woman—she seemed sincere. She was helpful, but I could see that she felt that she had her hands tied. Despite this, she sent the case to a rep. named Jeff Huart. He gave me the impression that this case was too small for him. While he was reading the Jack the Ripper Case Study I made, he asked me if I knew what I was being "charged" with. I said, "No." He said "come on, you know what they got you on they told you they saw the book." I said, "That didn't mean anything to me, I thought—." He cut me off. His cocky attitude turned me off from the jump. He then asked for me to leave the room so he could speak with Analia privately. Outside, in the lobby, I thought, I don't know if this guy is the enemy or the ally. I remember working at a nonprofit agency with a weak and helpless union that just took your money every month. From what I heard through the teaching channels, the UFT once caused fear in the DOE, but now they just seemed like rats running from the oncoming train. They took money from our paycheck but they gave us what? I sat there thinking if I was wasting my time.

The weight of the matter weighed on my mind. The door opened and the secretary informed me I could go back in Analia's office. John walked passed me and I and Analia spoke alone. She gave me the news that John would meet me the next day at the meeting. That was it. He couldn't even tell me to my face that he would "represent" me. I walked out more daunted than when I walked in.

CHAPTER 17: Due Process

On February 12, 2014, the "Due Process" hearing was held at 400 First Avenue. Me, Shelly, John Huart (UFT), and Susan Holtzman (Superintendent designee) attended. I met John outside the room. He advised me to let him do all the talking and just answer the questions, which was counterproductive to me because I sure as hell didn't need any other man to speak for me. But I relented (another lesson learned).

Before we walked in the meeting room, he stopped me and asked me about the note I wrote the previous day. I looked at him confused, "What note," I said. While sitting in Shelly's office the previous day I wrote the time I left on the sign out sheet to make sure I was paid for all of my hours. I also wrote, "sat all the time" from the time I got to her office till 2:50pm. John said, "She's saying that you wrote Satan." Now, I may not be a Christian or a Jew, but I sure as hell didn't release myself from the tethers of religion to re-enslave myself in a new religion! This is how diluted this administration had become.

As I entered the room I eyed Shelly sitting to the left of the rectangular table. Like usual, she fidgeted with her hands, which clasped together as if in a prayer visual. She had on some hideous turtleneck that distracted me from what was most important at the moment--but I wondered if she dressed like a Mormon intentionally?

At the short side of the table sat Susan. If the UFT reps were rats on the subway platform, she was the ringleader: I wanted to call her Master Splinter. She sat hunchback with a shawl over her shoulders. I felt sorry for her for no reason. Between her manlike shape and...Susan and Shelly spoke and I interjected "Good Morning". No response. Susan continued exchanging papers with Shelly as I sat down diagonally across from Shelly. John sat next to me and on the side of Susan. This whole situation smelt of a routine to me. I bet they did this everyday, shuffling good teachers out and harvesting the ones who bow down and do their filthy work. How many innocent pedagogues have passed through these chambers I thought. Yet with all their good intentions, their voices were lost among all the paperwork. How many voices have they succeeded in silencing in this office? - And how many will fall victim to the silence after me? To them, I deserved no more respect than a helpless child. It surprised them that I even knew how to enunciate letters in the alphabet and that I could say more than yes-mam. I'm that child whose opened his parent's bedroom door and discovered what's behind all the noise. In a quotidian manner, my knowledge will suffer the derogatory labels that the do-gooders often throw onto us to discredit us.

As I opened my mouth to describe the situation, my words fell on retarded ears. Susan and Jeff cut me off whenever I opened my mouth. I was like a Nazi taken before the Massad--there was no chance of a fair trial here. Before I made it halfway through my thought, Susan interjected to denounce my reply. With the few words that did manage to come out of my mouth Susan caught them and threw them back in my face. So long for this being an impartial meeting. I couldn't understand anything Susan said; she spoke nonsense and in circles. She opened her mouth only to make the meeting appear legitimate, but she had already made her mind up before I walked in the door. I stopped speaking halfway into the meeting, as my words were not going to be heard. This meeting was solely to record everything I said so they could demonize me in the end. If you are able to trick employees into believing that due process is fair, it makes being untruthful more easily—and the people don't challenge the process itself just because it implies that flowery word: equality. We believe we have a chance to make it, make it out alive. The joke is on us. For, those who make the rules are also those who break them. At the DOE truths stand in as lies and lies stand in as lies. For example, Susan's working relationship with Shelly stood as "legitimate" on account of their working titles--but both of these evil priestesses dabbled in untruths. I leaned over the table halfway through and directed myself towards Susan, "Why even speak any further, you two are obviously in cahoots with each other." She laughed then sighed, "Cedric, I'm listening but you're not telling me what I want to hear." All of this played out so routine for her.

As someone who's never been hauled into court, I imagined how so many black males must feel when standing before a judge who holds an unjust amount of power to manipulate their lives. As I sat across the table, I stared directly at my accuser, Shelly. She kept turning her head looking at anything but me. I knew right then and there how much power I had as one lowly worker and that I had put the fear of god in her: the ultimate weakness. All of her power and authority amounted to nothing when forced to confront me head on. But this is not a surprise, the education system and the labor market deals in cowardice. All those who want a safe normal life enter its gates that read: "Abandon all hope, all ye who enter here." (If we lived in the Wild Wild West, these are the same people who would hide in their homes like the pussies they are-- however, modernization and civilization have emboldened them and made them feel somehow worthy of the air they breathe.) Meanwhile, I debated how many people like me sat in this same seat, in this same position? How all of the actors in this room played their roles as if they performed justice. Was this justice? It was all an act. Susan denied all the valid issues I brought up--as if her marsupial looking ass was present when it occurred. Everything that came out of my mouth she responded to in a nasty and disrespectful tone. Her dislike of me showed on her pale face the moment I showed my black face. I think it was because that she probably thought my black ass couldn't construct a full sentence seeing as most of the members of the DOE administration are licensed illiterates!-And so can only imagine people equally asinine.

At this juncture, the real Cedric surfaced and I wanted both of them to have it. If this was a crisis and I was going down, I might as well interchange their judgment of me with my criticism of them. Before I got a chance to get some good emotional blows in, Jeff pulled me out of the room to speak privately. Outside, he berated me like some kind of child. The arrogance of both the DOE and UFT reps. shows that they have been "playing the game" so long that they believe it's real. I stopped him short before he scored a chance to see my alter ego, Cedrico! (Cedrico chews up and chews out any and everyone, including Cedric.) Jeff's whole attitude and demeanor smelled of treason. I couldn't put my finger on it why he worked with the DOE, but the UFT has been accused of worse. The DOE weren't the only jackals in the building. Jeff left me outside the room while he went inside to talk to Susan and Shelly privately. I heard yelling and then I heard laughing and each outburst chastised my patience. Why waste my time in this bureaucratic cycle of humiliation. I wanted to assume they were talking about the matter at hand, but a part of me knows they just had a laugh at my expense since they knew each other very well. I saw the whole thing unfolding in my mind, the secret dealings and negotiating-- I could imagine Jeff saying, "we will let you fire this guy, but you have to save one of our other employees."

I walked back into the room when John opened the door. We sat down. John looked defeated, Shelly looked scared, and Susan seemed happy to be a Superintendent Designee. Susan ordered me to report to the same building tomorrow morning at 8am. When I got outside into the brisk cold air I knew they would fire me, yet I breathed the sigh of a winner.

CHAPTER 18: Punishment and Reward

On February 13, I arrived at 400 First Avenue again and waited till Susan arrived. The days were still bitterly cold; New York experienced one of its coldest and harshest winters in some time and I felt somehow I came through the bitter season along with the cold. She came in about 840am and we took the elevator up to her floor. Her attitude acceded to a calmness that I shared with her. The fight was over.

As we arrived in her office she and we took our coats off, before I could even hang my coat around the chair she quickly said, "You're being discontinued, Cedric." Like that, clear and emotionless as when I first met her. I thought I heard a little joy in her voice. She wasn't amused by my confidence during the last meeting so she planned to evoke some emotional discharge by saying those words as hard as she did. But all I heard was the echo from her cold, hard lifeless heart. I imagined people like her and Shelly going home at night unable to even trigger the slightest volt of electricity in their most private parts, taking out their anger on their husbands for the life they're blessed with: a husband who couldn't probably get it up with two bottles of Viagra and a molly. You know the type! They come to work and take all their sexual frustration out on those poor people below them, who still remember what an orgasm feels like. Their money deposed their happiness so they resigned to remain so stale and frigid that money and power served no purpose. But, the more money they brought in the more heartache and the more rage they took home. Before long their faces fall hard and pale, and their jobs become their lovers. You know the type.

With open palms, I placed both hands on the table and leaned over and looked at her and said, "That's fine." Her blow impacted me in the slightest way; I was surprised somewhat, there was not one sting of conscience. When you've gravitated in bullshit for so long, you never grow to learn how a state of repose feels. What I went through at the Department of Education spared me of self-contempt. I congratulated myself. I realized just how fear operated--off of our belief; our belief in loss is the root of all fear. I realized I couldn't lose. It's worth saying again--I can't lose!

Susan handed me the discontinuance letter from the Superintendent. In the office, I sat thinking how the tradition of work and its knuckle down honor system was lost on me now. I was more than pleased about my transgression. Civil Disobedience sanctifies a righteous conscious. It wasn't my choice; it was my duty as an outlier, as an exception, as the zeitgeist of my age—to those who miscarry the belief in a life sans slavery. "The harvest is plentiful, but the laborers are few. "Virtue, if it still existed, would be solely granted to the man unashamed of the statement, " Under a government which imprisons any unjustly, the true place for a just man is also a prison." Without guilt or embarrassment, I exalt my offenses towards the administration at 226M as not only justice, but I wish I had done more to degrade and defile their taste--it was my duty to humiliate them in front of their "subordinates" to show once and for all that fear is an illusion. They couldn't do anything to me that had not already been done to me before. I hate when people say, "all of this was meant to happen because blah blah blah..." But, anyone who has known me since a young age can see a pattern--it took me thirty-two years to acknowledge this pattern, accept it and use it to my benefit. Based on my experience, harassment of an outlier like m would not have abated in the future, but instead matured had I not finally got off of my knees and kicked them hence. Humiliation draws no accommodations here. There are those who will say, it's good that he was laid off for his behavior was foolish; he didn't know his place! Know this: my good sense told me without needed assurances from any one else or any cosigner that life would provide a place for me, just for me--and it wasn't in that class. Isolated, I disconnected from my former self and demarcated my life as limitless. Shelly intended for that dungeon to fragment my personality, yet, it only served to make my resolve all the more unbreakable. That office they housed me in, where the district sends all of the "disobedient" teachers, was a place where teachers were sent to learn their lesson for their insubordination or lack of piety to the gods (management). I contemplate that Henry David Thoreau encountered government bodies like this when he wrote, "there will never be a really free and enlightened State, until the State comes to recognize the individual as a higher and independent power, from which all its own power and authority are derived, and treats him accordingly." (htt11)

Reflecting on the matter, I have determined in the future to entertain even more appalling literature. Damnit, I never learn!

February 13, 2014

Name: Cedric Hines File #:------

Dear Mr. Hines,

You have been assigned to Citywide Programs District Office located at 400 First Avenue, New York, NY 10010, 5th Floor to work with Assistant Superintendent Ms. Helen Kaufman. Your work hours will be 8:00 AM. to 2:50 P.M. Your designated lunch hour will be 12:00 pm to 12:50 pm. You are required to punch in and out in the AM. and P.M., as well as your lunch hour. The time clock is located on the 1st floor.

On March 14, at the end of the day, submit your timecard to MaryAnn Lucatorto at 400 First Avenue, New York, NY 1001 O-Room 661. All lateness and absences should be called in to Ms. Lucatorto at 212-802-1539 no later than the start of the work day.

Sincerely,

Catherine Ammirati Director of Human Resources

C: Helen Kaufman

CHAPTER 19: Redemption

At my work site I looked too comfortable next to Helen's office, the Assistant Superintendent for District 75, so they moved me to another desk among other workers on the same floor. Everyone walked by and wondered if I were a new employee and I would smile and act like I belonged and to anyone who enquired I would say, "I'm punished and made an example of," garnering a few chuckles. To me, it was funny. These sorts of situations in the past used to have a slight effect on me after I violated some rule. I thought about the things I would lose because of my salacious tongue. But, this time I conceived of all I could gain and the possibilities seemed as deep as the sea. Why did I take this job in the first place? I knew the position occupied itself with order and mundane achievement—something totally opposed to my way of life. Before I took on this chore, I wrote a blog post about taking a job with the government and how anything government means bureaucratic, slow, and backwards. What did I expect to find? It's not easy to accept who you are when it goes against everything you were taught. Hey! Don't fault me, I grew up a Democrat and was raised a Christian.

At the age of 32 something drastically changed me; something I fought off for years. I retired my Christianity years ago, but even my political leanings engaged different platforms as a result of my experiences. I was not a Republican, but the Democratic Party didn't seem the same party to me either. Both nauseated me for the lies and the division they caused in our country. And, the whole faith and family shit, well, it's shit. Religious faith is the cause of all wars, yet politicians legislate endless laws to pronounce peace. Still, there is no peace.

In the dungeon at 400 First Ave., I happened to meet a middle aged Jamaican woman whose name I can't remember; but her spirit I can't forget. At a time when I languished in the midst of nothing but devils, she descended out of nowhere and punched me with the kindest words I heard all week, "Hi, there." You hear these words behind an insincere heart often in the workplace, but I believed her greeting and the smile that accompanied it. I responded, "Hi" and she started talking about how much she loved Pharell William's "Happy" song and that she couldn't get it out of her head. She went on and on about the song till she finally opened the video up on YouTube. "You know I should be working but oh well" she said, and we laughed because we both knew what that "oh well" signified. It was a small act of resistance to the life imposed on her and me. Her spirit wasn't dead yet. She avoided turning into that rigid devil many of others in the DOE worshipped.

She laughed with a full heart at the song and sang along with it and some of her coworkers, who still hung onto shreds of happiness, came and sang with her, forming a crescent shape around her desk and singing the chorus like a choir. I laughed with them and thought about their lives. I followed the thought and wondered how they fared; how did they suppress the troubles of this labor market everyday and how they overcame, if they were overcoming or just surviving like so many of their colleagues.

After the song ended, she dared to ask why Helen sat me there at that desk and I gave her a short and ambivalent answer. She read right through me, lifted her head to the sky while clasping her hands together and said "You know, god puts us through certain things and we don't know why", and she went on about her god and her faith and I couldn't help think to myself how long the people would hold onto that fable. It saddened me even more that the words dropped out of the mouth of a woman so full of life and vigor--but I couldn't get passed the thought that her whole life would be a waiting game, a story without an ending.

I rose from my seat looking down on the Jamaican lady and went to the bathroom. I thought about how many have come before her with the same dreams and the same unfulfilled wishes? My heart sank. The sad truth is that those at the bottom have the most faith because they have nothing else. This is the way they fight. I maintained the urge to tell her that faith was not enough. Faith is a mistress of religion who couldn't care less about god. As long as believers get what they want, they believe. It's a selfish state of mind, but the people guard against admitting this for fear they resemble their exploiters. For at heart, lacking consideration for the basis of their faith, they prey and prey and prey to be above and beyond their fellow man. Believers are worse than their exploiters because they hide their inner desires behind holy garb. If they have to step on the backs of their fellow man to get that promotion at work, all the faith in the world couldn't stop them. In my estimation learning more about god leads one away

from god! For, Jesus himself worshipped an outright
revolutionary ideology then declared himself the one. If alive
today, he would consume a communist diet. And look how far
that system of thought got the beleaguered countries, which
unfortunately bear its economic mark. For many generations it
was dangerous to say state this fact: A faithless man is a wise
man. For the thought of trusting in one god alone should be
reason enough to cancel that faith. How could you think of only
one god when so many others stand in line to put their faith in
you? The working class has the most faith; a faith, which believes
if they trust in god, that one day they'll be the outliers. It could be
revolutionary, if it wasn't so damn much of the same ol' "fight the
power" rhetoric we've heard all of our lives. Religious people are
nothing other than the proletarians attempting to snatch victory
in a "next life" because they can't get it in this life. The situation
for us is so bad that we had to create another life to get over the
misery of living this life. Even faith today is losing its faith.

And to those who want more out of life, what are they fighting
for? -A car?-A house? -To survive one more day? It isn't enough.
What was I fighting for? -To save my job? -A job so inclined to
dismiss me and continue on as if I never existed, as if I never
mattered? I took a long, deep, unbiased look inside of myself and
saw my problem. For so long, I had been taught--but the student
was now the teacher still acting like a student. I knew that the
work place contended against our nature. I knew it repulsed me,
yet something kept holding me back. I knew how to fight, but
what I was missing was something to fight for; and when I looked
around there was nobody but me.

"Cedric, where are you going to look for a job? When are you
going to look for a job? How will you provide for yourself? Aren't
you scared? How will you survive?" I knew the sincerity of their
questions rested with themselves. They didn't know how they
could do it, but they wanted to watch me and see if it were
possible to escape this drudgery we call the labor market so that
maybe they might attempt it one day, one day escape it: modern
day slavery.

In the subtle and fiery words of Toni Morrison, "Freeing yourself
was one thing, claiming ownership of that freed self was
another." It was this day I vowed never to hassle myself in a job
anymore. I am more than that--I am all of that!

I searched all over the world to try to get away from it, but even as I travelled overseas, I discovered that the misery followed me wherever I landed. The working class is a universal problem! I've tried escaping it in the physical world, but now I've come to the stark light of reason, which tells me that the journey begins with the way I think. Traveling to Asia, Europe, South America or anywhere else can't free me. I had to change my mind about my predicament and act on that newfound energy! I had to cultivate, incorporate, and buy out my own mind; it behooves me to kick the old landowner to the curb and declare that this land—my mind—is mine and mine alone. On top of it, I'll build monuments towering above my tallest hope. In a way, my resistance helped me to liquidate my assets in this system and place them back in myself. Nobody, from this day on will reap profits from this machine, except me. No longer will the market consume, share, redefine, rent, mortgage, pawn, sell, exchange, transfer, give away, nor destroy my human capital.

=================

CERTIFIED RETURN RECEIPT# 7003 2260 0004 9595 3164

March 17, 2013

Cedric Hines

Dear Mr. Hines:

This is to inform you that I have received no documentation from you in response to my letter of discontinuance dated February 12, 2014. I reaffirm your Discontinuance of Probationary Service and termination effective close of business March 14, 2014.

Sincerely,

Gary Hecht, Superintendent District 75
C: Charles Peeples Francine Perkins-Colon Theresity Smith Nelson Serrano JoAnn Rabot Catherine Ammirati Rachel Klainberg

=====================

CHAPTER 20: Class Dismissed

July 2014, I received a voicemail and email from the UFT Special Representative Mary Atkinson.

Hello Mr. Hines,

You visited the UFT several months ago to appeal your discontinuance. At the time, we also filed a legal intake to ask our attorneys to review your case. They have just informed us that based on their review, they don't believe they would be successful in challenging your discontinuance in court. However, you can file on your own or with a private attorney. If you intend to pursue this on your own (or with your own attorney, which is recommended), you should do it as soon as you possibly can since there is a time limit involved. I am attaching a copy of a sample notice of claim to challenge your discontinuance to give you an idea of what needs to be filed. You can serve the notice of claim by taking it to the NYC Corporation Counsel office, also known as the Law Department, at 100 Church Street in Manhattan. You should ask for directions when you get to the building for the exact office in the building that accepts the filing of a notice of claim. I wish you the best in your efforts.

Thank you,

Mary Atkinson
UFT Special Representative
Manhattan Borough Office
=====================
How could the same government, which often inflicts the most harm on us, somehow come to my rescue? -The same government that legally lynches us and writes us off as deserving; the same government that catalyzes the ignorance that pushes me to the brink of insanity. If it were not for this government with increasing tentacles across the globe, maybe I might have gotten away before now. Are we talking about the same government that reaches in my pockets and takes everything I have and walks away leaving me penniless and broken? I should beseech it for help? It is my curse--and it is ever my wish to see it fall to its feeble knees and beg forgiveness. This government, I know it very well. It's well paid and paid off! It is a lie and was the first lie implanted on this soil. In its name we have fought,

and shed so much blood, for so much money, stealing so much time. I know what settles its appetite, more blood and more dollars. I found it out a long time ago when I saw it at the alter preying to itself and I asked who was god anyway? And it said, "I am." I've seen its first love and I counted her lovely also, if she weren't so damn useless; she could be of so much more beauty and vivaciousness, but it put her out on the market to please itself. It causes so much pain and strife in the world.

Knowing this, I did everything in my power to get fired. How many people truly reach their true potential at a job? The 9-5 is the modern day slavery and if it sounds like hyperbole to you-- well, you've proven who you are in the hierarchy of life. The labor market sucks you dry of every last drop of resistance you have, and believe it or not resistance is the first chemical of human nature. We came about from resistance, from the crashing of rocks together out in space, to the atoms that crashed into each other in the ocean to create the first living creature. Life came about out of resistance, yet the new world would have us discipline ourselves to believe that its peace that keeps the world turning. Energy is the cause and the most uncooperative energy. And we are no different from the space dust that inspires life. Like these particles, I unconsciously set myself free. I took shots at the power structure that existed even before I was born; I laughed in the face of authority; I didn't walk with my head down and I stared them in the damn eye: I didn't know how to be a slave.

Self-actualization irradiates you the more you dare to take the most inappropriate steps. Crash into people with the force of a comet. At its best, life is inappropriate. No! I won't behave. Appropriate behavior, such as saying "Yes-sir" and "yes-mam," is incompatible to the taste of my tongue, which should prefer the sweeter words (e.g., perineum)--and all of you sons of bitches who disagree, can lick mine! When you try to turn a lion into a cat all you see is pussy! Compatible to any circumstance is the behavior that shocks and awes not that behavior which dances to the same old tune. Those who turn their backs on the old ways of respect have my utmost respect. I fly over and above those who feel it their duty to pay homage to another man. Other men are prevalent more so than the foam in the sea, they are nothing or nobody to be honored. No man will ever get me on my knees-unless it's a form of foreplay! No! I won't behave. A man is compatible to me when he can cause the two strips on my zipper to open before the two on my mouth, or.... Any other sort is unworthy of a cursory glance. "Appropriate" is the only word that should come under censorship--that and "family values." Appropriate: meaning, made for chumps. From my very youth, I have been inappropriate in the eyes of these chumps: teachers, professors, managers, etc. It's a sign of enfranchisement to be labeled inappropriate.

The Superintendent was correct: my actions were egregious and appalling. For there was no way to truly become myself and escape class bondage, which I was born under, unless I escaped and transcended the beliefs of the working class! For so long they have come to believe what upper class people thought of them: that, "They have no morals." But, the middle class' cup overfloweth with morals. It's the upper class that has shed their morals and claimed otherwise. They enjoy luxuries and extravagances more so than the world has ever known and they show out in our face. However, here lies the middle class still in its dying days trying to appear upright: going to church every Sunday; believing in the god concept; trusting in the community when the individual is clearly the most important component of the world; trusting in what CNN and their nightly news feeds them--from the same corporations owned by the upper class! The jig is up. Or is it?

The working class (caste) refuses to help itself. Countless authors write books about their situation; directors have filmed movies about their situation; the news reports are flooded with examples of their situation. Nevertheless, they continue find joy in the least: being humble is what they call it. They have convinced themselves, by their values, that their struggle is actually noble! LOL. As if going to work, killing yourself for $8.95/Hr was noble. "Work," they say, "is respectable." But there's nothing respectable about dying from overtime! The constant and ever cloud of fear hanging over the office place, until this day, cast on the people, undetected, negative health effects that have long range and far reaching implications for our children and for our future.

This is a warning: Dare not try to help them or they'll turn on you and strike you. There's nothing like being woke from a delightful dream into a miserable reality. Speak a new slogan: that selfishness is altruism. The people stand pitted against each other. As anger grows at those who manipulate and take their lives for granted, they can't help but still remain envious and hateful of their fellow man. Their altruism is what eats at them-- that steady and constant obligation to care for the fellow man. Look at the man on the subway who feels compelled to get up when an elderly or pregnant woman walks onto the train! Look at the anger on the faces of people who must rise for the family and all the children! I say, each and every one of us individuals should practice the art of altruism and let them stand! Lacking consideration for others is not immoral, it's serves the greater good. Those with strong healthy appetites for life are the most selfish people; it's because they consider themselves first that they don't walk in secret maliciousness towards their fellow man. I'd rather be in the midst of Dick Cheney than Hillary Clinton, for fear she might resent me for having to bow to my lowly level to garner my vote. And Dick, well, we know he just takes what he wants.

I've learned that if everyone would mind his or her fucking business, the world would be a better place. (Look at my situation--I had no business outing Shelly, Imma, or Jeanne for their illegal and/or unethical deeds; for, in truth, I think what irritated me most about the administration was that they possessed so many of the same qualities I have.) But people are too busy trying to escape their proper place, when they don't have the inner strength to withstand the storm that is created by resistance. What are we left with? -The disgruntled masses who turn on those who attempt to help them. They are the same people who go to work and say I just want to get my paycheck and not get involved in any workplace politics--including Union activities. They don't want to "shame' themselves by associating themselves with people who work on behalf of the people. They think they are safe if they just keep their mouths shut and do what the master orders On the contrary, I stood in shame everyday. I spoke back when I knew from the deepest parts of my bowels that employers or educators were trying to pull the wool over my eyes. Nevertheless it's not the masses fault they can't see past their misery. The prospect for the future looks like a nightmare. And think not that I believe the working class serves no purpose; they serve the greatest purpose; slaves are needed just as rulers are! Slaves provide the backbone of the nation, whereby the wealthy can enjoy the life they deserve. Just think what kind of monstrous generation we would usher in if everyone acted like individualist? -I.e. acted as their true selves. (I say acted because some go against their inner natures attempting to be individuals when in reality they just want to please other people). So we find the wealthy are entitled to their wealth solely on account of their rich values: selfishness, individualism, and violence. They don't ask for what they want, they take it. They don't cry foul; they launch wars. They don't ask for permission... We individualist denounce the "social instinct" in America. If we deem everyone acceptable, who would fill the places of the "undesirables?" The caste system in America needs and thrives off of a permanent underclass. Even with all of its advances and progress, only so many live freely: that is, past the limits of subsistence.

If your lucky, you realize that like Dorothy in the Wizard of OZ that you could have went home at anytime with the click of your heels, or better yet, by changing your mind about the social instinct--to stop harassing and belittling the 1% who claim themselves for themselves--who truly appropriate behavior. They take behavior for themselves and redefine it. They are aware that the boogieman doesn't exist and he isn't coming back to exact revenge on the wealthy.

The class remaking of New York City's Department of Education, and America as a whole, will last as long as the need to be acceptable is in fashion.

CLASS DISMISSED
================
P.S.
But, even those working class people with different identities and politics, even they still hold tight to their working class values! It's their values I hate most! Forced on them by higher society, the working class forced their values onto me. And they enjoy their misery (i.e., their family values). I don't! As a result, the people are clay for the higher classes to mold; before long, they harden and solidify into a work of art and act as if their creation was divine, when it was an experiment in social control.
Until the day, when the people rise up for--instead of against the individual, I say,

FUCK THIS CLASS!

Supporting Documents

From: Hines Cedric
Sent: Monday, October 28, 2013 12:35 PM
To: Klainberg Rachelle (75M226)
Subject: RE: IEP Review (STUDENT)

Hi,
Sorry for the late reply, I just saw the first part of your email. I
can talk now 1216-107pm and also 158-243pm (coteaching
session).

_____

From: Klainberg Rachelle (75M226)
Sent: Monday, October 28, 2013 6:22 AM
To: Hines Cedric
Subject: Re: IEP Review (STUDENT)

Also, for (STUDENT), you must fax in the attendance page
before the document can be finalized, once reviewed. Rebecca
will do this for (STUDENT) triennial. Ask a veteran teacher at the
site if you don't know how to do this.

Shelly Klainberg
Principal
P226M
212-477-5017

From: Klainberg Rachelle (75M226)
Sent: Monday, October 28, 2013 06:20 AM
To: Hines Cedric
Subject: Re: IEP Review (STUDENT)

Hi Cedric --
Here are my review notes. Please make sure Rebecca is not
finalizing the IEPuntil corrections are made. Most notes will
need to be fixed on all IEPs, so make the same changes for
(STUDENT) and let me know when you have finished so I can
review. I think we can go deeper with the content of your
academic goals. I'll give you a call later today. When would be a
good time? I'm working on the issue with the need for a BIP not
coming up on the Summary page....

Present level-
-discuss why (STUDENT) requires a crisis para.

Goals:
-2nd OT goal -- last objective incomplete
-No Social Skills goal
-Reading, writing, and math goals -- Let's touch base today about content.

Recommended programs and sevices:
-List special class as "D75 Schools" (do this on 12 month service page, too).
-projected start date for all services should be 10 school days after the date of the IEP meeting.
-APE is 3 times per week - I changed this for you.

-Participation in assessments -- list as reason that (STUDENT) academic functioning level is too low for participation.

-Participation with students without disabilities:
-under "Explain the extent".....write that "(STUDENT) will participate in all classes within his special education program."
-under "If the student is not participating in regular physical education..." Write that (STUDENT) will participate in Adapted Physical Education 3 times per week."

Shelly Klainberg
Principal
P226M
212-477-5017

From: Hines Cedric
Sent: Thursday, October 24, 2013 09:40 PM
To: Klainberg Rachelle (75M226)
Subject: IEP Review (STUDENT)

Hi Shelly,

I have completed (STUDENT) IEP. However, when I check the "compare with previous document" page, it shows that (STUDENT) does not need a BIP, when in fact, he does. I don't know how to correct it.

(STUDENT) IEP is finalized. I just have to check in with the Helpdesk about an issue with his Prior Written Notice package. I'll do that first thing in the morning. The only change I made was to make his math objective quantities "up to" 5, 10, 20 --- it didn't make sense that all sums would equal the same amount. I also added the language of his Social Skills objective into his PLEP.

(STUDENT) -- take one more look at the social skills goal -- the 2nd and 3ed objectives are almost the same. Please revise the third objective. You also need to include how he will demonstrate these skills -- by selecting from an array of photos? Once you modify this, you can tell Rebecca it is ready to be finalized.

Shelly Klainberg
Principal
P226M
212-477-5017

From: Hines Cedric
Sent: Thursday, November 14, 2013 1:45 PM
To: Klainberg Rachelle (75M226)
Subject: RE: IEPs

Hi,
If you'll be there all day, I can call at 250pm, if that's okay?

From: Klainberg Rachelle (75M226)
Sent: Thursday, November 14, 2013 9:58 AM
To: Hines Cedric
Subject: Re: IEPs

Please disregard --- I had edited this to say 76, but the original message apparently sent, too. I'll be at 76.

Shelly Klainberg

Principal
P226M
212-477-5017

----- Original Message -----
From: Klainberg Rachelle (75M226)
Sent: Thursday, November 14, 2013 09:42 AM
To: Hines Cedric
Subject: Re: IEPs

Can you call me at 208 at noon?

Shelly Klainberg
Principal
P226M
212-477-5017

----- Original Message -----
From: Hines Cedric
Sent: Thursday, November 14, 2013 09:29 AM
To: Klainberg Rachelle (75M226)
Subject: RE: IEPs

Shelly,
Will you be around anytime today? I would like to bring some
ideas I have about (STUDENTS) and (STUDENTS) IEP's to the
table. Im aware that (STUDENT) IEP is due by tomorrow in
terms of compliance, but it's very important we are in agreement
about the goals. Let me know.

Cedric

From: Klainberg Rachelle (75M226)
Sent: Thursday, November 14, 2013 6:06 AM
To: Hines Cedric
Subject: IEPs

Hi Cedric....we're almost there.

In your Present Levels of Performance, don't write out your

entire goal. Just indicate the general goal areas students will be working on next -- "(STUDENT) next steps are to add dollar and coin amounts up to $10, measure the length of objects using standard and non-standard tools......" or to "examine texts by narrating and sequencing events, and providing a personal response to what he has read.". I have question about his Math goal. It's a very big jump to go from coin identification to add coins up to $10 --- that's a lot of coins. Are you sure that's a reasonable objective?

Please edit your Present Levels, email me when done, and I will finalize today.
==============
PARENT LETTER
From: (PARENT]
Sent: Tuesday, September 17, 2013 2:27 PM
To: Hines Cedric
Cc: (PARENT)
Subject: (STUDENT) as ASD student

Cedric,

It was nice to meet you yesterday under the circumstances of the bus. As I mentioned, (STUDENT) has had 4 teachers in 4 years; no one's fault, just the way life is.

About a year ago we learned that our son is a math genius one end, understands 4-5 languages (self-taught; YouTube has been good to him), but as non-verbal has trouble with 2-way communications. He often gets frustrated if he is bored.

So what has happened the last 4 years, each new teacher begins (STUDENT) with some basics, like counting pennies and coins, what shape is what and what shape is bigger, and many other elementary stuff that he has done long ago. When he can crank out (he does need a prompt from his mother; a touch on the wrist) he does some math that is amazing in both speed and complexity.

He can crank out (less than a second) 827 x 385 and gives the answer; fractions squared by fractions; square roots; and other college-level, even MBA math. So when I said he's intelligent I am not comparing him to any other student, special or normal

Because of the communication barrier and prompting (we are working on both) his real off-the-charts intelligence is being held back, not nurtured. The last teacher he had quit giving (STUDENT) homework 9 months ago and he was excellent in math.

See attached homework that he does with his mother. He's impressive in terms of speed and the fact that no one has even really taught him, other than to show him a process. Once he gets how a problem is done, he never has to be taught a second time. Call him savant, or whatever, but he's unique with social deficits in many ways.

Finally, when he tested for the angle (is he measuring obtuse or acute) he does it with his eyes to the exact degree: 161, 37, 87, 94, etc... He does that with no protractor or compass, like the rest of us used to measure with back in high school.

So if he displays boredom or dis-interest in class, it's because he has done something so simple before, he is asking himself, why am I doing 2x2 again, size of shapes, etc. He has been doing that type of low level (for him) problem solving since 2005. At 13 years old, he is beyond that.

So, in the opinion of his parents, your homework assignments should be focused on social studies and English. Leave the math a lone. He is doing calculus and trigonometry now with GMAT book for MBA college grads.

Any questions, contact (PARENT) or I.

Regards,(PARENT)

PARENT LETTER

From: (PARENT]
Sent: Wednesday, November 06, 2013 1:12 PM
To: Hines Cedric
Cc: (PARENT)

Subject: (STUDENTS) behavior

Hi Cedric,

Some background info first:
(STUDENT) has gone through puberty already, so that angst stage with emotional crying in the morning and aggressive behavior (scratching is what he did last year) has passed by. Several years ago, we put (STUDENTo on a medication (3 months) that made his OCD worst. When he was a child of 3 years old, receiving his ABA treatment he became excellent in eye contact and being prompted for every little thing.

To this day, even at home, he will ask/seek permission on prompting for everything. Even playing computer to even doing his math homework--1 question, 1 prompt, 1 answer in a split second.

This issue of prompting, he becoming independent has been a challenge or us and even a psychologist we paid last year. If you have any ideas other how to make that fade away, he would test much better and perhaps behavior will change too.

In 4 years, he has had 4 teachers. Just the way it is sometimes. So each new school year he starts from scratch all over again.

He is bored or tired, he can be a problem, from poor behavior to shutting out with great disinterest. So that too is a challenge.

Let us know your thoughts.

Regards, Parent

SOURCES

HTT-Peter Meyer. "New York City's Education Battles: The Mayor, the schools, and the "rinky-dink candy store"." Education Next. Spring 2008/Vol. 8, No.2(http://educationnext.org/new-york-citys-education-battles/)

HTT1- Race: The power of an Illusion. (http://www.pbs.org/race/000_About/002_04-background-02-12.htm)

HTT2- Devin Dwyer. "Post-Racial America? Not Yet, Civil Rights Legend Andrew Young Says." ABC News. May 25, 2010. (http://abcnews.go.com/Politics/andrew-young-civil-rights-legend-book-race-politics/story?id=10731590)

HTT3-Leonard Greene. "NBA owner to sell team after racist email." New York Post. September 7, 2014. (http://nypost.com/2014/09/07/atlanta-hawks-owner-to-sell-team-after-self-reporting-racist-email/)

HTT4-comrade glowstick. "Labor in Communist Society." The Red Star Vanguard. June 12, 2012. (http://theredstarvanguard.wordpress.com/2011/06/12/labor-in-communist-society/)

HTT5- Sharon Lerner. "Teachers Left Behind." The American Prospect. May 15, 2013. (http://prospect.org/article/teachers-left-behind)

HTT6-Al Baker and Marc Santora. "No Deal on Teacher Evaluations; City Risks Losing $450 Million." January 17, 2013. (http://www.nytimes.com/2013/01/18/nyregion/new-york-city-talks-on-teacher-evaluations.html)

HTT7-Philissa Cramer. "State releases outline of evaluation system it's imposing on NYC." June 1, 2013. (http://ny.chalkbeat.org/2013/06/01/state-releases-outline-of-evaluation-system-its-imposing-on-nyc/#.VDHzYCldXv8)

WWW/WWW1: www.stopcommoncoreny.com

HTT8- "Debate: Should Schools Embrace The Common Core? September 19,2014. (http://www.npr.org/

2014/09/19/347145921/debate-should-schools-embrace-the-common-core)

HTT9- Joseph Jacobs. "English Fairy Tales: Jack and the Beanstalk."(http://www.authorama.com/english-fairy-tales-15.html)

HTT10-"Mainstreaming vs.Inclusion." Knox College. (http://faculty.knox.edu/jvanderg/201_Website_S_08/Inclusion.html)

HTT11-H.D. Thoreau. "Resistance to Civil Government." (http://sniggle.net/TPL/index5.php?entry=rtcg)

HTT12-"Rejection of Irish Teacher Highlights South Korean Xenophobia." The Guardian. November 7, 2014. (http://www.theguardian.com/world/2014/nov/07/irish-teacher-south-korea-xenophobia-alcoholism)

BALDWIN-James Baldwin. The Fire Next Time. Vintage; Reissue edition (December 1, 1992)

EDWARDS- June Edwards. Opposing Censorship in Public Schools: Religion, Morality, and Literature. Routledge (December 1, 1997)

About the Author

Sir Cedric is a global citizen originally hailing from the San Francisco Bay Area. After graduating from the University of California, Davis, with a degree in Political Science, he took a trip to New York City, found the city pleasantly inappropriate, and decided to call the location home. Cedric graduated with a Masters in Public Administration from Baruch College and immediately began working on his upcoming book, *Laissez-Faire.* In the interim, Cedric wrote *Fuck This Class!* and continues to devote his time to living life on his own terms in spite of the plebs.

Sir Cedric writes for:
cedricfucksuptheclassics.com

facebook.com/**cedric.hines.7**

www.ingramcontent.com/pod-product-compliance
Lightning Source LLC
Chambersburg PA
CBHW052103090426
42739CB00010B/2300